TALIESIN ORIGINS

EXPLORING THE MYTH
OF THE GREATEST CELTIC BARD

GWILYM MORUS-BAIRD

 Dr Gwilym Morus-Baird is a musician, researcher and tutor of courses on Celtic myth. He has released several albums of Welsh language music and was one of the founding members of Eos, the Welsh broadcasting rights society. He studied Welsh literature at university and completed a doctorate in the mediaevel Welsh bardic tradition. He lives in Gwynedd with his wife and children. His lectures, videos, podcasts and online courses can be found at celticsource.online.

This book can be followed as an online course with additional materials, video and — more importantly — group discussion. The live course is led by Gwilym Morus-Baird and runs several times a year. The video version of the course is always available and can be followed at your own pace. You are very welcome to join us.

Visit *https://celticsource.online/taliesin-origins*

Yn gyflwynedig i Tomos a Melys.

Er cof am Tony Conran,

athro achlysurol a chyfaill cyson i mi

yn ystod fy mlynyddoedd yn y brifysgol.

Fe'm darbwyllodd i gadw'r ysbryd ar ei echel.

Acknowledgements

Special thanks to Mike Jones for suggesting I throw the first draft on the compost and rewrite the whole thing. Many thanks to those who read the early drafts of this book: Adam Thorogood, Ann Beer, Simon H. Lilly and Ceitidh Carw for your patience, wise insights and error corrections. This is for you:

Darllenydd

Rwy'n ddall i rai o 'ngwallau, ac angen

Dy gyngor a'i olau.

Yn nhywyllwch llinellau

Gwelir rhodd dy eglurhau.

Reader

I'm blind to some of my errors, and need

Your council and its light.

In the darkness of lines

The gift of your clarifying is seen.

All remaining errors are very much my own.

Thanks to Natalia Junqueira for designing the cover I always wanted, and to National Museum Wales for permission to use that stunning photo of the spiral shield boss from Tal-y-llyn.

Many thanks to the Celtic Source community for attending courses, discussing, questioning and generally having a great time. Many of the insights here were refined in class with you all. Keep it up, please! You make my work inspiring.

With love and thanks to my beautiful wife for telling me to take a break and giving me space and support, and our kids for being awesome. A very special thanks to Anne and Mike for being my favourite in-laws and supporting our family in so many ways. You really are the best.

Contents

Pronunciation

My mother tongue is beautiful. Yet for anyone unfortunate enough to have never heard its tones and rhythms, like any new language, it can look a little daunting on the page. But I encourage you to try to move your tongue and mouth in these very old ways. It's so easy to let strange words remain unfamiliar and contribute to the weird evolution that often occurs when non-native speakers try to say Celtic names without guidance. There is always an inevitable evolution as words emigrate into new languages, but just so that we can all be on the same page as much as possible, please give the pronunciation guides a try. Every time a new Welsh word appears in the text, I've given as approximate an English equivalent as I can in the footnotes. These guides will never be totally accurate but they will get you very close. Just pretend you're reading an English word and it should make sense.

In the guides themselves, the CAPitalised SYLLables are where you place the main accent in the word. There's no English equivalent to the Welsh 'll', so I've simply left it in the guides.

It's pronounced by holding the tongue in the final position of 'l', drawing the lips back a little as if you were pronouncing 'ee' and blowing down the sides of the tongue, not in a harsh or forced spitting sound, but gently and cleanly. We also have a 'dd' which is equivalent to the harder 'th' in 'they'. But we also have the softer 'th' sound as in 'think'. So check how the Welsh word is spelled: if it's a 'dd', the guide is referring to the heavier, if it's 'th', it's the softer. We also roll our 'r's, and 'ch' is like the sound in 'loch'. I've recorded many of the more common Welsh names in Celtic myth and you can listen to them at the website: https://celticsource.online/resources/

Introduction

It was a small, hardback notebook with parchment-like pages, bound in an orange cloth with a Chinese dragon printed on the cover. It smelled faintly of incense. My mother had given it to me as a Christmas present and it had instantly become my little repository of adolescent secrets. I couldn't have been much older than thirteen, and in that transformative year I had begun to write small scraps of poetry, tangled and confused lines in both Welsh and English. One of my clearest memories of school that year is drifting about the busy playground, clutching that little cloth-bound notebook. I felt overwhelmed by an intense feeling that something needed to be said, but not knowing quite how to say it.

My imagination was already a fantastical place, overflowing as it was with a potent mix of *Mabinogion* and *Lord of the Rings*. The images I set down in that rough poetry were full of wonder. I was truly enchanted; *tipyn o freuddwydiwr* ('a bit of a dreamer') as the teachers would say. I distinctly remember scratching out a brief sequence of 'I have been . . .' lines, a list of transformations that probably included things like 'I have been a book; I have been a dragon; I have been a star . . .' and so on; a heady brew of adolescent fantasy drawn straight from the poetry of the legendary Taliesin,[1] the mystic hero of Welsh folklore. I must have come across him at some point in my education, but I can't for the life of me remember when I first heard of his myth.

I thought I still had that little orange notebook with the Chinese dragon on the cover, but for all my searching, I found nothing. It should have been in an old box of tapes and mini discs. I could see it clearly in my mind's eye, yet all I found were some old car tax forms. It still hasn't turned up. I'm not sure how long I stayed enraptured by the Taliesin spirit, but a fascination with that very traditional Welsh myth has never been that far away. I always seem to return to Taliesin.

The other significant memory I have of immersing myself in his poetry was the year I finished my A-levels. I was eighteen and had finally bought myself a copy of *Canu Taliesin*, the standard edition of the great bard's historical poetry. I was initially dismayed at how difficult it was (it was written in ancient Welsh), never mind how utterly different to the more fantastical poetry of the later sixteenth-century legend. It really wasn't what I had been expecting; it disheartened me how

---

1   Tal-YES-in.

long it was going to take to figure out this archaic poetry. But within a few weeks, I had grasped the meaning of the first few poems and although I didn't really find them that interesting, I appreciated the history they belonged to. That's another book I can't find, lost somewhere between here and my first days at university.

After leaving home for the first time, I did the usual thing, exploring the vices and pleasures of university life and spending more money than I had (the local bank manager had rolled her eyes). It was also the first time I got to immerse myself in a relatively well-stocked university library. One cold winter morning, I sat on the floor beside the history section with a small pile of books on Welsh history. I already had a loose grasp of the subject, but I found the details fascinating. It was here that I began to appreciate the full breadth of what we might call 'the Taliesin tradition', to borrow a phrase.[2] It was the first time I really grasped how broad and ancient the Taliesin myth was, how it comprised many written sources, from the earliest heroic poetry of the sixth century to the folktale of the sixteenth and beyond.

Over the following weeks I went further (by now using a desk like a normal student) and realised that many of the themes in Taliesin's myth had an even more ancient origin. Like everyone lucky enough to have a good Welsh language

---

2   See Emyr Humphreys, *The Taliesin Tradition* (Black Raven 1983).

education, I had known since childhood that as one of the Cymry,[3] the Welsh, I was descended from the Celts of the Iron Age. In ancient Britain, these tribes spoke the Brythonic language through to the end of the Roman occupation. This was when I first made the connection between the Druids, the historical Taliesin of the sixth century, the court bards of mediaevel Wales and the early modern legend about the mystic bard. I felt like I had uncovered some great ancient secret. Of course, as I came to appreciate later, Celtic scholars had been making these connections for about a century before I was even born.

But in my moment of realisation, I felt like I had been touched by some divine inspiration, given a potent vision of my own Welsh tradition. The distant past suddenly sped towards me at such great speed it made me dizzy. The story I thought I was uncovering for the first time had both heroes and villains, underdogs and oppressors, magic, war and mystic visions. Like any other young Welsh person alive in the 1990s, I had an implicit understanding of cultural politics. Wales was mostly English-speaking and only in certain places did Cymraeg[4] remain the majority language. We were always in the shadow of the greater Anglo-American culture that strode across the world stage like some giant, gleaming pop-star. But

---

3   KUM-ri.

4   Kum-RAIG. The Welsh language.

in those early days of student life, I saw that the designation of my people as a 'minority culture' hadn't originated in the English state. The fight for cultural integrity had been going on for a thousand years before the Normans even arrived on British shores. In my explorations of Welsh history, I began to appreciate that it was, in fact, a very old tale that had its roots in a time before we were even known as Cymry.

Perhaps the most significant event in the history of the Iron Age Celts was the Roman invasion. By the turn of the first millennium, the Roman Republic had spread beyond its native territory in present-day Italy and colonised many lands around the Mediterranean Sea. Two centuries later, it was an empire that had conquered almost all of north-western Europe, including most of Britain, slaughtering and enslaving millions of Celts along the way.[5] Roman violence and governance, the projection of both military and cultural power, ultimately brought about a transformation in Celtic civilisation. We can guess that there were greater degrees of Roman influence in the cities and towns and less in the *pagus* ('countryside') amongst the *paganus* ('those of the countryside'), but most of the power in Celtic hands accrued to those willing to negotiate their bondage with the all-powerful Roman state. I now understood how this story had turned into my own time,

---

5   In his *Commentaries on the Gallic Wars* (58 BCE), Caesar claims that out of 3 million Gauls, one third was killed and another third was enslaved. In his *Life of Caesar*, Plutarch, a Roman philosopher of the first century CE, confirms these figures.

the great narrative wheel rolling through its many episodes, returning to its beginning several times before turning to this modern era. Just as we had been free many times, we had just as often lived under one tyranny or another.

I gave up on my first attempt at university after a year. I was too restless (and probably too arrogant) to listen to lectures. I had my own plans and they involved a guitar. It took another decade before I was ready to try university again, and by that time I had a much clearer idea about how I was going to do it and why. I had eventually realised that my 'unique' flash of inspiration was but a spark to the roaring fires of knowledge that had been burning in Welsh academia for centuries. Historians had been arguing for some time about the problems of early Celtic history, and in the face of so much intense discourse, I took my first nibble of humble pie. I questioned what exactly I was after. I knew that my chief passion was being a musician, performing, writing and recording, but I was also drawn to something in my people's ancient culture. Over time, I realised it was something far more nebulous, far more mysterious than simply chasing down the cold facts of the historical record. It took some time, but eventually, thanks to some French philosophy and modern poetry, I had a name for my passion: symbolic meaning. In very simple terms, this is the deeper, broader, more foundational meaning of poems and stories; what could also be called myth. Throughout the following years of research, I kept getting glimpses of an evolving mythology, a body of enigmatic narratives that explored a range of philosophies in symbolic form. It was interpreting those symbolic meanings that captivated me, not so much studying the history they arose from.

I had known since my teens that the more interesting strands of Welsh mythology were preserved in mediaevel literature, and only some guesses can be made as to how much of that had been inherited from the Druids. Apart from a few brief words written in letters borrowed from other people, the most important Celtic remains that survive the Iron Age comprise enigmatic images carved in stone and sculpted in metal. The Celts were mainly an oral culture, preferring the spoken word and memory to writing. As a result, historians rely heavily on the works of Greeks and Romans for contemporary accounts.

The problem with these classical sources is that their authors were looking at the Celts from the outside. The Romans typically saw them as barbarians they had either already conquered or were in the process of doing so. With an aggressor's eye, it was in their interests to dehumanise the Celts, to portray them as wild savages in need of civilising by a morally superior culture. We therefore have to take what these authors say with a pinch of salt. Some scholars do not trust their testimony at all because much of it probably served as propaganda to justify invading resource-rich territories. Others believe that, although we must be careful when we consider these classical sources, they at least suggest what the Celts were like in the late Iron Age. When other evidence is so scarce, it makes no real sense to ignore these accounts of Celtic culture.[6]

Soon after beginning my second attempt at university, I realised I would never be the traditional type of academic who maintains the rare but precious culture of Welsh language higher education. I was far too undisciplined to take on the more technical aspects of middle Welsh grammar and the peculiarities of mediaeval orthography. As a musician living on the wild side of life, I saw university mainly as another source of income that happened to let me pursue my personal interests in Celtic myth and the Welsh bardic tradition. Foolishly, I thought I was just signing up to use the library, when in reality, it turned out I also thoroughly enjoyed the lectures. For some reason, the School of Welsh at my university were kind enough to let me stay on and complete a master's and doctorate in subjects that actually kept me paying attention. I finally got around to learning the basics of Middle Welsh and picked up a healthy scepticism. I am immensely grateful to the lecturers

---

6   This is a long running debate in Celtic scholarship. I tend to agree with the common sense of the 'no-smoke-without-fire' position taken by Prof. Phillip Freeman in his paper 'Classical Ethnography and the Celts: Can We Trust the Sources?', *Proceedings of the Harvard Celtic Colloquium*, Vol. 20/21 (2000/2001), 22-28. A more sceptical but thorough account is given by Ronald Hutton in the first chapter of *Blood and Mistletoe: The History of the Druids in Britain* (Yale, 2011), 21-108.

and supervisors who guided that often tactless and vacant young man through the various disciplines of the academy. I consider those years precious, and with the distance of time I can appreciate how fortunate I was to pursue several years of research in something I really loved.

By the end of my studies I had come to some of my own conclusions. There must have been some continuity between the Brythonic druids of the Iron Age and the Welsh bards of post-Roman Britain. What exactly had been inherited? It's difficult to say specifically, but I kept catching glimpses of common themes in both periods. Although not explicitly named as such, the early Welsh bards were a type of priest class: they claimed access to a divine power (called awen, literally 'inspiration') which they expressed in public ceremonies of praise for the living and commemoration of the dead; even though they only dealt with one Christian deity, their ceremonies were still redolent with a powerful, quasi-religious heroic mythology; they were versed in different types of oral literature, including poetry, mythology, history and ancient lore; they appeared to be a special class of the nobility, and even though they may not necessarily have been born to the aristocracy, their long years of training gave them high status.

Perhaps crucially, even though they were Christians, they also appeared to maintain a belief in the transmigration or reincarnation of the soul. All of these themes are embodied in the mythic Taliesin, and as we shall see, it's in his mediaevel mythology that they find their full expression. This is an important distinction, because even though the ancient Iron Age roots of this mythology will be considered, it's the mediaevel flourishing that I'll be focusing on. That is, after all, the most potent version of the myth to have survived.

Since finishing at university and slowly but surely coming to a more leisurely pace in my music career, I've had the opportunity to teach my chosen subject privately, online, to many people from across the English speaking world. Teaching is one of the most valuable things any lifelong student can do. If you care about the subject, as I do, taking on the responsibility of guiding others into the country, showing them the sights, helping them avoid the dead-ends and introducing them to the unmapped regions, makes you not only consolidate what you know but also makes you reconsider it as you seek to make it meaningful to others. Particularly for those who weren't fortunate enough to have been raised and educated in this rich and ancient culture, I've tried to consider how best the sources, materials and history can be presented.

This book explores all the most important stories and poems that make up the Welsh myth of Taliesin. As you would expect, it therefore covers a lot of history, but this isn't strictly a book about history. It's a book about a myth: a vast and tangled myth that spans millennia and contains many characters, locations and texts. Some sources might be familiar to some readers, while others will be new to almost everyone outside of a Celtic Studies department. Yet even with the more popularly known poems and stories there are new aspects, concepts and themes explored, deeper parts of the myth and more subtle elements of the tradition considered.

It's also worth pointing out that parts of this book will be very speculative. Old myths show more than they tell; their meaning is implied rather than explicitly stated; they're more symbolic than literal. This means myths need to be interpreted before they can be fully understood, and interpretation is by no means a hard science. If anything, it's more of an art; a creative process of finding patterns, comparisons, suggestions and inferences. That's not to say that I haven't been as careful as I can be when looking at historical sources. Some of the older Welsh texts discussed in this book are ambiguous and often difficult to understand, even for the most experienced scholars. Our knowledge of the past is naturally incomplete, and every generation is ultimately constrained by its own historical perspective. There is no way we can perfectly understand what the ancient peoples of Wales meant by their myths.

But I do believe that we can get close to understanding what these myths could have meant, while also allowing that these interpretations will inevitably be anchored in our own age. Humans have evolved little in the last few tens of thousands of years. We still experience the same basic drives, instincts, reactions, and feelings. We still fall in and out of love, get jealous, angry, and fear death. I believe we can still recognise the basic human experience that's reflected in old stories, and when we need to fill in the gaps, we just need to use a little common sense.

In addition, fortunately for us, far more accurate editions of the primary sources have been published in recent decades, with copious notes to help us find the breadcrumbs in the dark woods. We now understand many of these texts far better than we ever have, and there are several that we need to consider if we are to fully appreciate the long evolution of Taliesin's myth. Perhaps the most important is the mediaevel manuscript known as *The Book of Taliesin*, created sometime around 1325 CE. Our best guess is that it was copied by a professional scribe working at the abbey of Abaty Cwm Hir[7] in Mid Wales. We don't know who the scribe was nor who employed them to produce this compilation of Taliesin-related poetry. There would have been traditions concerning Taliesin circulating in the area in the early fourteenth century and an archive of Taliesin-related material may have already been kept in the abbey's archive. The scribe may also have drawn on manuscripts borrowed from other places, using the network of professional copyists, court bards, and clergy to seek out those

---

7   Ab-AT-ee Coom Heer; 'oo' as in 'book' not 'soon'.

works that were most closely associated with the legendary bard. After its completion, the book would certainly have been of great value to professional poets, preserving as it did poetry attributed to one of the more important founding fathers of their tradition.

Most of the poems discussed in this book are preserved in *The Book of Taliesin*: either those believed to be composed by the historical sixth-century Taliesin, or those by later bards working in his voice, usually composed in the period between the eleventh and fourteenth centuries. It has taken almost a century and a half for Welsh scholarship to produce reliable translations of many of these poems, largely because they can be incredibly ambiguous, never mind intentionally archaic and obscure. Long decades of work by diligent researchers were needed to understand them as well as we do today. In 2007, Marged Haycock published her groundbreaking edition and translation of the legendary poems from *The Book of Taliesin*, providing for the first time a reliable and accessible edition that could be used by both laypeople and scholars alike. As a result, the many errors in the translations that came before Haycock can now be clearly seen. Those published by J. Gwenogvryn Evans in 1915 and by W.F. Skene in 1868, in particular, should now be set aside by all serious researchers and authors. Unfortunately, perhaps because they are freely available online, many continue to make use of these poor translations, and perhaps worse, sometimes develop theories based on such unstable foundations. I have given up counting the amount of times I've seen modern druidry books use these very flawed translations, and the responsibility for pointing out these glaring errors shouldn't rest on the shoulders of Welsh scholars and researchers. We have more important work to do. If Anglo-American druid organisations and groups wish to draw on the traditions and primary sources of Welsh culture, they should take the utmost care in doing so. There is no excuse and hasn't been for a few decades now.

One last story from my college years, if I may. Having been raised in a mainly Welsh speaking culture, I was largely ignorant of the significant influence the Taliesin myth had on the modern Anglo-American subcultures of druidry, witchcraft and paganism. I had caught glimpses of this influence, but I had never truly appreciated how substantial it was. To me, a modern druid was a Methodist minister or college professor who wore a white robe at the National Eisteddfod.[8] But at university, hidden amongst the scholarly works and authoritative editions, I came across brightly coloured books covered in swirling designs and shamanic symbols. This was my first real exposure to the other type of modern druidry, that which had been evolving for at least two centuries across the border in England. To be frank,

---

8   Ay-STETH-vod; 'ay' as in 'hay'. The largest cultural festival in Wales presided over by an order of modern-day Welsh druids.

I was mortally offended. The first thought that came into my naïve young brain was that the English had taken so much from us, how dare they take this? Was there nothing left sacred that the Welsh could claim as their own? I spent months trawling obscure internet forums and messaging boards, trying to understand exactly what had been stolen and how it was being used. I unfortunately met some rather polite and interesting people that were too nice for me to get really angry with; they were largely oblivious to the cultural politics of what they were engaged in. A few could empathise and others were sensitive to the situation, but as far as most were concerned, Taliesin was just as legible in English as he was in Welsh. The eternal transformer was surely having a laugh.[9]

It took some years for my feelings to change. As I ventured into my doctoral research, I had started reading modern anthropology and found it a powerful tool for understanding the more ambiguous workings of mythology in culture and society. This interest eventually led me down many paths, some of which ended in ceremonies and rituals held by indigenous teachers from different parts of the world. The medicine people of Turtle Island, in particular, seemed to have some precious advice and, when I was ready to hear it, it was very simple. It really boiled down to the question, do I want to live at war or in peace? The cultural conflict I felt honour bound to pursue

---

9 If you haven't already, you should get this joke about half-way through Chapter 7.

was in fact a war that raged inside myself. The adversary I had identified was a face painted on all the historical injustices committed against my people, and no matter how factually true all of that was, that war would eventually tear me apart. Sure, there are those who will appropriate and misinterpret, strip-mining other people's cultural treasures for their own profit, but the truth is most people aren't like that. The transgressors are actually quite few, and the remaining majority are just every-day folks trying to find some meaning in this mad and modern world. In my experience, almost all the people who attend my courses are careful, diligent and sensitive, wanting to see these traditions for what they are, not some second-hand fantasy version. I remember sitting in front of a large fire in a tipi about fifteen years ago now, listening to Navaho songs accompanied by drum and rattle, and thinking to myself how much more I could get done if I acted out of peace instead of rage. It felt like I was returning to the native pacifism of my Nonconformist ancestors. Who knew they would feel so at home in front of that fire? I can confidently say that this book is written in the spirit of peace. I hope you can receive it in the same way.

CHAPTER 1

The Tale of Taliesin

According to the opinion of the people . . .

This tale does not begin in the ancient groves of Môn,[10] nor the soaring crags of Eryri,[11] nor the deep valleys of Y Rhondda.[12] It begins on the French coast, at Calais, when that ancient port was still occupied by England. In 1530, the city and surrounding lands had been part of England for two centuries, but it was the last foothold in a once expansive territory within France. Henry VIII had been king for two decades and was trying to get rid of his first wife, butting heads with Rome over his attempts to annul the marriage and carrying on with ladies in waiting. In the same year, a Welshman by the name of Elis Gruffydd[13] arrived at the harbour of Calais and entered the

---

10   Mawn; 'aw' as in 'lawn'. Anglesey in English.

11   Air-UR-i. Snowdon in English.

12   RHON-tha.

13   GRIF-ith. Some sources say he arrives in 1529.

walled city through the Lantern Gate. He had taken work as a soldier in the English army garrisoned there.

Like many of his fellow countryfolk, Gruffydd had made the best of a world where the Welsh were a conquered people. During the following decade of the 1530s, Henry VIII would seek to consolidate English dominance over Wales and further impress upon the Welsh nobility that their future was in fashionable London, not the backwards culture of their homeland. England had conquered Wales in 1282 and the following centuries of struggle and revolt had only resulted in harsher English measures and ultimately apartheid for the Welsh. By the turn of the 1500s, the bad old days of the independence struggle were long over, and men like Elis Gruffydd had got the message that speaking English, not Welsh, was how one got on in the world.

Yet Gruffydd was a man of two worlds: to all appearances, he abided by the realpolitik of English cultural hegemony, even glorying in the battles fought and won by his fellow English soldiers; but his writing reveals an internal world that revolved around the great myths and legends of his native Wales. Before arriving at Calais, he had been in service to a nobleman in London, a role that gave him enough leisure time to pursue his interests with relish. It was in London that his love of Welsh literature flourished into a copious collection of texts copied into a large tome with a quick and tidy hand. Writing in his mother tongue in these texts, Gruffydd shows himself to be an erudite and objective thinker, broad and ranging in his interests, yet firmly rooted in the soil of his native culture. By the time he arrived at Calais, he was ready to embark on a much greater work of his own devising.

By 1532, Henry VIII was making eyes at the French king, Francis I. The two regents met at Calais that year, Henry seeking support for the annulment of his marriage and Francis seeing if he could turn the English king's dislike of Rome to his own ends. By the same year, Elis Gruffydd had clearly found his feet at Calais garrison. While the kings and their courts bathed in their opulence, Gruffydd was working on the first parts of what would become over the following decades one of the most detailed accounts of world history ever written in the Welsh language, his great masterpiece, *Cronicl o Wech Oesoedd y Byd* ('The Chronicle of the Six Ages of the World').

Although following a contemporary style in historical writing, drawing on English scholars in particular, his work was naturally imbued with a rather Welsh perspective. As a result, Gruffydd's *Cronicl* not only covers the major events in world history as commonly understood at this period, but also many episodes and accounts from the rich culture of Wales. Amongst the myriad stories and legends Gruffydd recorded, we find the earliest complete version of *Ystoria Taliesin* ('The Tale of Taliesin'). At the time, it was one of the most popular folktales amongst the Cymry, and had been told up and down the country for countless generations. Snippets of the tale can be found in the poetry of earlier centuries, and not just in the rustic verses of the common folk, but in the classical poetry composed at the highest levels of Welsh society. The Taliesin myth seemed to have permeated the whole of Welsh culture, both high and low, and it was the most natural thing in the world for Gruffydd to include it in his Welsh history of everything. What follows is a translation from his *Cronicl*, slightly adapted for the modern reader:

The Tale of Taliesin[14]

When King Arthur was just beginning his career [sometime towards the end of the fifth century], there was a nobleman living in the land called Penllyn.[15] He was called Tegid Foel,[16] and according to the story, his inherited home was the body of water we call Llyn Tegid[17] ['Tegid Lake'].[18] He had a wife called Ceridwen,[19] whom the writing says was skilled and learned in the three arts, namely magic, witchcraft and sorcery. Tegid and

---

14   The commonly used Welsh title is *Hanes Taliesin*. My translation of the text in Patrick K. Ford, *Ystoria Taliesin* (UWP 1992).

15   PEN-llin.

16   TEG-id Voil.

17   Llin TEG-id.

18   Bala Lake in English.

19   Ker-ID-wen.

Ceridwen had a son, and he was very unpleasant in form and face and behaviour, and he was called Morfran.[20] Ultimately, because he was so dark, he was named Y Fagddu[21] [or Afagddu, 'Utter Darkness'].

And because of his ugliness, his mother was full of sorrow: it was clear that her son would never have a place amongst the nobility unless he had other virtues beyond his appearance. And so as to bring this about, she meditated upon her arts to see how she could fill him with the spirit of prophecy and make him a great storyteller about the world to come. And after labouring long at her arts, she saw how this type of knowledge could be achieved through the virtues of the Earth's plants and human effort. That was, to gather a large variety of plants at certain days and hours and put them all in a large cauldron of water, then put the cauldron on a fire, keeping it at a constant heat, and boil it day and night for a year and a day, after which time three drops of the essence of the many plants would be ready. They would cause whatever person these three drops fell upon to be supremely knowledgeable in many arts and possess the spirit of prophecy. The remaining liquid would be the strongest poison in the world and break the cauldron to pieces and release the poison upon the Earth.

---

20   MOR-vran; 'o' as in 'not'.

21   Ur VAG-thee.

And truly, this story is irrational and against faith and sanctity! But the story reveals she gathered a great many of the Earth's plants, and these she put in a cauldron of water that she put on the fire. And she took an old blind man to stir the cauldron and boil it. To the boy who guided the blind man — Gwion Bach[22] — Ceridwen gave the task of keeping the fire below the cauldron. And in this way, each one performed his task as well as the other: keeping the fire and boiling the cauldron and stirring it, and Ceridwen keeping it full of water and plants until the end of one year and a day.

Then Ceridwen took Morfran, her son, and put him close to the boiling potion, ready to receive the drops when the hour came for them to leap out of the cauldron. Then Ceridwen set her backside down to rest, and she happened to fall asleep at the very moment the three virtuous drops leapt out of the cauldron. These fell on Gwion Bach, who had shoved Morfran out of the way. And with that, the cauldron cried out and broke with the strength of the poison. And with that, Ceridwen woke from her sleep like a madwoman. Gwion — who was replete with knowledge — saw clearly that her wrath was such that she would kill him in an instant, and that she knew he had stolen the virtuous drops. For this reason, he took to his feet and fled. The instant Ceridwen's wrath subsided, she asked her son what had happened, who told her the entire story of how

---

22   GWI-on Bach; 'ch' as in 'loch'.

Gwion had shoved him out of the way. So she dashed out of her house and after Gwion Bach, and as the story shows, she saw him escaping quickly in the form of a hare. Because of this, she transformed herself into a black greyhound bitch and chased him back and forth. And in the end, after long pursuit in many forms, she was so intent on him she made him flee into a barn where there was a gigantic pile of winnowed wheat and he transformed himself into one grain. What did Ceridwen do but transform into a short-tailed black hen and swallowed Gwion into her womb, where she bore him for nine months, about which time she gave birth to him.

But when she looked upon him, newly born, she couldn't in her heart do him harm by her own hand, nor allow any other to harm him in her sight. And in the end she put him in a coracle or skin bag and made it snug. Some of the books show she cast him in the lake, yet others say into a river he was thrown, and others say she threw him in the sea in the place he was later found. When the time came, he returned as the following tale here shows.

The Story of Finding Taliesin

When Maelgwn Gwynedd[23] was holding court in the castle of Deganwy,[24] the saintly man called Cybi[25] was living in the

---

23 MILE-gwn GWYN-eth.

24 De-GAN-we.

25 CUB-i; 'u' as in 'cup'.

land of Môn. And also at this time, a wealthy squire lived beside Deganwy Fort, who, as the story shows, was called Gwyddno Garanhir.[26] He had a fish-weir on the shore of the Conwy[27] close to the sea, in which ten pounds worth of salmon was to be had every Nos Galan Gaeaf[28] ['Winter Eve Night']. Gwyddno had a son called Elffin,[29] who was in service at the court of king Maelgwn. And the writing shows that Elffin was a generous nobleman, loved amongst his companions. But he was a lavish and prodigal son, as were most of the courtiers. While things were good for Gwyddno, Elffin had no need of money to spend with his companions. And as Gwyddno's riches lessened, he stopped giving his son money, who complained to his companions that he could not fund their socialising and companionship as he had done before, because his father had fallen into poverty.

Nevertheless, as before, he requested some courtiers ask [his father] for the fish from the weir as a gift for him after the next Nos Galan Gaeaf, which is what they did, and Gwyddno allowed the request. And so when the day and the time came, Elffin took several servants with him to wait at the weir, which he guarded before the tide until after it ebbed. When Elffin and

---

26 GWITH-no Gar-AN-heer.

27 CON-we.

28 Naws GAL-an GAY-av; 'aw' as in 'lawn'. Halloween. October 31st, the last day of the old Celtic year. Samhain in the Irish tradition.

29 ELF-in.

his people came into the fish-weir, they saw neither head nor tail of a single minnow. The weir was usually overflowing on that night, but Elffin saw nothing but shadows.

So he lowered his head and began bemoaning his misfortune as he turned away, claiming that he was the unluckiest man in the entire world. But in that moment, he was determined to find something and so returned to search for anything in the weir, and before long, he found a coracle or skin bag. Then he took his knife and cut the skin, revealing the forehead of a child. And the instant Elffin saw the brow, he said: 'Behold a fair brow!' In other words, a 'shining brow'. Upon those words the child answered from the coracle 'Taliesin it is!'[30]

According to the opinion of the people this was the spirit of Gwion Bach, who had been in the belly of Ceridwen, who after giving birth to him threw him in the water or in the sea where he wandered from the time of Arthur to about the beginning of Maelgwn's, which was about forty years.

This is indeed far from reason or sense. Nevertheless, as before, I will follow the story that tells of Elffin taking the bag and putting it in a basket on the back of one of his horses, and in that place Taliesin declaimed the verses called 'Elffin's Reward', like this:

---

30   Tal = brow; iesin = radiant, shining.

Fair Elffin, stop your weeping;

Hoping for the worst will do no good.

Never was anything better had in Gwyddno's weir

Than [what was found] this evening.

With many other verses, he sang for Elffin's enjoyment along the way home. Before long, Elffin delivered his prize to his wife, who raised him well with tenderness.

This first part of Taliesin's legend is then followed by further episodes in which the young bard grows into a formidable young man, besting the court poets of Maelgwn's court and rescuing his patron, Elffin, from misfortune. But it's this first part that contains the more significant elements of the myth, turning as it does about the central figure of Ceridwen and her role not only as a destroyer and mother but also as the keeper of the mystic cauldron of awen.

Elis Gruffydd's tale, perhaps set down by him sometime around the 1540s, is the first of several versions of the folktale to appear in the historical record. The later versions tell a similar story, but are most notably set in other parts of Wales. One early and significant version was recorded by the antiquary and collector John Jones of Gellilyfdy in 1607, but in his version the nameless babe isn't set adrift upon the River Conwy in North Wales and found in a weir close to its estuary, but is cast upon the Dyfi[31] River in Mid Wales and found on the nearby beach of Borth,[32] which is significant when we consider that the ancient name of the place was *Porth Wyddno*, the 'Port of Gwyddno', Elffin's father in the tale. When Borth Beach was recently surveyed by an archaeological team from Lampeter University, they found an ancient fish weir of oaken stakes buried under the sands.

There are other geographical factors that make John Jones' version interesting, such as a beach in the estuary called Traeth[33] Maelgwn, 'Maelgwn's Beach'; or the fact that the source of the Dyfi River, a small mountain tarn called Creiglyn Dyfi,[34] being only a few miles from Llyn Tegid, Ceridwen's home in both of the earliest versions. Or that the Dyfi Estuary is overlooked by Bedd Taliesin,[35] 'Taliesin's Grave', an old burial mound that has borne the legendary bard's name for several hundred years at least.

John Jones' 1607 version is also the earliest to mention the three animal transformations:

---

31   DOVE-i.

32   BORTH; 'o' as in 'song'.

33   Trithe; 'th' as in 'think'.

34   CRAIG-lin DOVE-i.

35   BATHE Tal-YES-in.

. . . and she ran after him, and he saw her and transformed into a hare while running, and then she transformed into a greyhound and caused him to swerve and turned him towards the River Aerwen, so he leaped into the river and transformed into a fish, and she as an otter sought him below the water, until it was unavoidable for him to do nothing but transform into a bird for the sky, and she a hawk pursued him and did not give him respite in the air . . . [36]

The other significant difference in Jones' versions is that Gwion Bach apparently receives the three drops by accident, not through any malice, giving a slightly different meaning to the tale. Neither does Jones record as many events after Elffin's discovery and naming of Taliesin.

But both Gruffydd and Jones are telling the same basic story and preserving the same common myth, told far and wide by both high and low-born Welsh. And neither do both authors simply refer to the tale in passing. Gruffydd gives as full an account as he can, clearly drawing on external sources and searching out the verses for the different episodes of the story. It was no minor tale included as an afterthought, but an important myth that lay at the heart of the Welsh culture of his time. He could not tell the full story of world history without including it in all its magic and wonder.

---

36 My translation of the text in Patrick K. Ford (ed.), *Ystoria Taliesin* (UWP 1992), 134.

Yet neither could Gruffydd simply recount the tale. He also included his own critique of the stranger parts, particularly those sections he believed were 'irrational and against faith and sanctity!' He was conscious of his responsibility to maintain certain standards. Gruffydd clearly saw himself as a historian assessing the veracity of his sources, and where they diverged from the cultural norms of early modern scholarship, norms heavily influenced by the Church, he was duty bound to call out the 'irrational' and reveal the limitations of the materials he was drawing upon. Gruffydd was not a mystic, even if his fascination with traditional prophecy could lead us to think otherwise. From within the culture of his own time, he was seeking to maintain the highest standard of scholarship, and as a result, his version is not that of folk culture or common belief, but of a compiler of history. To search out what mythological strands and folk beliefs are preserved in his version, we must turn to other comparative sources.

During the last years of Gruffydd's work on his *Cronicl*, the wheel of history continued to turn. Henry VIII continued to plough through wives like birthday cakes and tried a few times to regain territory in France. But even though his French schemes bore little fruit, at home he had successfully bound Wales ever tighter to England with the Acts of Union, making independence impossible to even imagine for almost half a millennium and banning the Welsh language from the corridors of power and the courts of law. The educated Welsh, particularly those in service to the English crown, became further embedded in that establishment, drifting further from their cultural roots. Many intentionally neglected their native tongue and often kept little more than their Welsh names. This period became known as *Brad yr Uchelwyr* in Welsh history, the 'Betrayal of the Nobility', an acknowledgement by the monoglot folk of common Wales that their 'betters' had largely abandoned them to their poverty and disenfranchisement and taken more luxurious apartments in England.

Yet despite the dramatic anglicising of the upper classes, the folk culture of Wales, rooted as it was in one of the oldest languages in north-western Europe, persisted and is given voice in the historical record through the many stories, poems and legends set down not under the patronage of the absent nobility, but by enthusiasts and lay folk like Elis Gruffydd — the soldier of Calais — who, far from home, would return time and again to the words and visions of his own native culture.

CHAPTER 2

The Taliesin of the Tale

Upon those words the child answered

from the coracle 'Taliesin it is!'

O f course, there would be no tale had there been no Taliesin. It is a legend about one of the founding fathers of the Welsh bardic tradition, the historical Taliesin, who lived during the last half of the sixth century. Unfortunately, most of what we can say about him is pure conjecture, based as it is on various modern readings of archaic poetry. But in bringing together these frayed threads of history, we can at least guess at what the ancient tapestry once looked like. He lived at a time just after a dramatic shift in the Celtic culture of Britain, when the Welsh language had just evolved out of the earlier Brythonic tongue that had been spoken on the island for a millennium or more.

In the year 410 CE — over a century before Taliesin's birth — Roman control of Britain ended when the last officials of the Empire were apparently expelled. Britain descended into further turmoil as different invaders sought to capture territory from the early Welsh, whose ancestors had inhabited the island for at least two thousand years before the Romans had arrived.[37] During the remaining decades of the 400s, Germanic chiefs increased their small foothold on the southern and eastern shores, Picts continued their raiding from the north and the Irish from the west, and in the middle of it all the early Welsh kingdoms were still trying to find their feet in the vacuum left by the collapsing Roman Empire. It was under these pressures that Cymraeg[38] evolved, perhaps developing alongside a revitalised identity for the ancient Brythonic people who would now come to call themselves Cymry,[39] the native inhabitants of Britain. The first half of the 500s was just as unsettled, and Taliesin was born into a time when the Welsh and Germanic tribes were fighting it out over who would be dominant south of Hadrian's Wall.

The first mention we have of Taliesin in the historical record is in the *Historia Brittonum*, a brief account of British history written in Latin in 828 CE. In an entry for the middle of the sixth century, it tells us:

---

37 I am following here a relatively new theory in Celtic history which argues the Celtic language evolved in Britain and elsewhere on the Atlantic seaboard. For a summary, see Barry Cunliffe's chapter 'The Arrival of the Indo-European Languages' in his book *The Ancient Celts* (OUP 2018).

38 Kum-RAIG. 'Welsh'.

39 Literally 'People of the same place'.

Then Talhaearn, Father of Awen, and Neirin and Taliesin and Blwchfardd and Cian, who is called Gwenith Gwawd, together at the same time were renowned in British poetry.[40]

British here, of course, means the early Welsh. The shift in language that followed the departure of the Romans may have not only revitalised the Brythonic identity but also the ancient bardic tradition of these Celtic people. Talhaearn, the first poet mentioned in the list, is called the father of awen, and this may simply have been a sign of his own sense of grandeur or perhaps it was a more meaningful title: was he the founder of a new bardic order? The 'father' of a new lineage in the native arts? The 'Tal' that makes up the first part of his name is of course the same 'Tal' that we find in Taliesin, but whereas Talhaearn means 'iron brow', Taliesin means 'shining' or 'radiant brow'. Although an explicit reason is given for the meaning of Taliesin's name in the later folk tale, was it originally regarding some type of metalwork worn on the head? The idea of an iron-foreheaded bard and a shining-foreheaded bard in the same generation is suggestive. Or is this referring to a spiritual light shining from the brow, not that dissimilar to a saint's halo? A similar light is described elsewhere in the Celtic tradition in the story of *The Death of Cuchulain*.[41] There is at least a

---

40   J. A. Giles (ed.), *Six Old English Chronicles* (London 1848).

41   T.P. Cross & C.H. Slover (eds.), *Ancient Irish Tales* (Barnes & Noble 1996), 338.

connection between the names of these two bards: Talhaearn being the father of awen and Taliesin, one of the better known bards of a new generation working in an ancient tradition.

Modern scholarship has generally accepted (although not unanimously) twelve early Welsh poems as the work of the historical Taliesin, even though they appear to have been copied down in the ninth century. One theory is that the original core of these twelve poems may well have been composed by the sixth-century Taliesin and was then preserved in the oral tradition of the Welsh bards. As a result, these poems would have slowly evolved by being reworked and updated by successive generations, and finally written down in the ninth or tenth centuries.[42]

Taking for granted that these twelve poems are at least close to the work of the sixth-century Taliesin, a rough outline of his life was suggested by the editor of these poems, Sir Ifor Williams. According to Sir Ifor, Taliesin was probably born somewhere in Mid Wales during the first half of the sixth century, and would have served his apprenticeship under the tutelage of a *pencerdd*,[43] or 'chief of the bardic craft'. As part of his training, he would have memorised many poems, stories, histories and lore, and trained in the specialised techniques of Welsh bardic poetry. The most important part of his education

---

42 Janet Davies, *The Welsh Language* (UWP 2014), 22-3.

43 PEN-kerth.

would have involved learning how to compose and perform praise poetry for the Welsh nobility. He probably spent his early career praising the local chieftains of Powys before advancing to praise the higher-ranking nobility.

If there is any truth in the account given by Elis Gruffydd of Taliesin's youth, he may have been a precocious young talent who visited the court of the historical Maelgwn Gwynedd. Traditionally, Maelgwn's chief court was at Deganwy, and overlooked the Conwy estuary on the coast of North Wales, but he's also connected with several places across the country, including Traeth Maelgwn ('Maelgwn's Beach') in the Dyfi Estuary just north of Borth, where in one version of the folktale the as-yet-unnamed Taliesin washes ashore. One tradition tells of how Maelgwn finally succumbed to a 'yellow fever' — almost certainly the Justinian Plague — in 547 CE while trying to isolate himself in a church. If any of that is reliable, then Taliesin could have been born in the 520s or 530s. If he was in training as a young apprentice bard at this time, it's quite possible his *pencerdd* took him along on a visit to a great king's court. High-ranking bards often visited the courts of important kings with apprentices in tow, either while on circuit throughout the land or perhaps on some formal business on behalf of another king.

And it's at the court of another Welsh king that Taliesin may have begun his official career. Sir Ifor Williams suggested that perhaps the earliest of Taliesin's poems to have survived was composed for Cynan Garwyn,[44] the king of Powys.[45] According to the poem, Cynan had given generous patronage to the young bard:

A hundred horses as fast as each other	with silver harnesses.
A hundred purple cloaks,	each as broad as the other.
A hundred bracelets for my arms,	fifty expensive ornaments.[46]

For such a price, a young poet was likely to say anything that would make his king happy. We know little about Cynan's actual military career, but the poem mentions victories against the men of Gwent, Môn, and Dyfed.[47] All of these battles were against other significant Welsh powers of the day, to the south, the south-west, and the north-west of Powys. But no mention is ever made of the ascendant power of the Saxons to the east nor the Angles to the north-east. This may have been a period of truce or even collaboration; plenty of later Welsh kings whose territories bordered those of the invaders had no issue with making alliances if they aligned with their own interests. But neither is any mention made of Rheged,[48] the Welsh kingdom

---

44 KUN-an GAR-win; 'a' as in 'bad' not 'car'.

45 Ifor Williams, *Canu Taliesin* (UWP 1960), xvi-ii.

46 My translation of the text in Williams (1960), 1.

47 DOVE-ed.

48 RHEG-ed; 'g' as in 'get'.

of Yr Hen Ogledd[49] ('The Old North'). The one poem we have in praise of Cynan is silent about the only other Welsh power worth mentioning at this time.

We can only guess at why Taliesin left Cynan's court in Powys and travelled north. The bard may have found the king's reluctance to fight the Saxons — the most significant threat of the age — an issue, made even more distasteful because Cynan instead made gains by attacking his own people. Not that Cynan was in any way unique in his attacks on other Welsh kingdoms; all the tribal powers of post-Roman Britain were in a long and permanent state of conflict with each other, regardless of ethnicity. But a trained bard like Taliesin would have appreciated the history and ethnic unity of the Welsh as one people, and therefore perhaps had a greater sensitivity to the very obvious impending danger from the east. The Welsh had lost significant territories over the preceding century and continued to do so at an alarming rate throughout the 500s. That historical reality may have cast Cynan in a rather unfavourable light, and Taliesin may not have wished to be damned by association. Another reason may well have been that the young bard simply didn't think Cynan would ever really make anything of himself, and if Taliesin was to fulfil his ambition of creating a poetry that would sing down the ages — the dream of every aspiring bard — he needed an object

---

49   Ur Hain OG-leth.

of praise that could inspire him to reach such lofty heights. He may have realised he needed to attach himself to a man of greater vision.

There are many reasons a young bard such as Taliesin may have headed for Yr Hen Ogledd and the kingdom of Rheged. The only certainty is that the exercise of his bardic art would have been central to his decision. Someone who had spent years dedicating themselves to such a practice, one that bestowed rare privileges on those fortunate enough to have been trained in its ways, would not have wished to squander either that dedication or opportunity. The very craft that enabled Taliesin to travel across the Welsh kingdoms was also the cause and the final destination of his journey. The famed Urien, king of Rheged, would become the object of his awen-infused attention.

When he left, it's doubtful he went alone. The shifting boundaries of tribal territories, the persistent raids and skirmishes, the collapsing of some kingdoms and the expansion of others — sometimes within a matter of a few years — would have made the journey north a difficult one to judge. If Cynan's gifts were real, Taliesin could well afford to take some apprentices at least, as well as retain a few fighters, guides and fixers for the long journey. As they travelled north from Powys, they would have stayed within the band of Welsh territories that stretched from what's now the West Midlands and Cheshire up to present day Lancashire and Cumbria, as far as the Solway Firth and perhaps further.

Cynan's court was at Pengwern,[50] present day Shrewsbury, and an old Roman road headed north to the ancient walled city of Deva Vitrix, or Chester as it's known today. In Taliesin's time, this was still an active stronghold held by the descendants of the Romano-British, and being only a few days' ride north, it was probably the most obvious destination to head to first. They would have passed either directly through or close by Chester, fording the Dyfrdwy,[51] 'The Waters of the Holy One', somewhere to the south of the walled city. From there he may have followed the western coast, a route long used by Celts and Romans alike, turning north with the seashore and only coming inland again as the Ribble Estuary pressed them eastwards towards the crossing at Preston.

There were several Christian settlements in the area, and being a member of the new faith, Taliesin would have visited some of the more important establishments. He may have paid his respects at the 'Matrona' shrine, an ancient pagan stone altar once dedicated to the earlier mother goddesses, then appropriated by the Christians and re-dedicated instead to the great Christian mother goddess, Mary.

---

50   Pen-GWAIRN.

51   DOVE-r-doo-i. The River Dee.

The Welsh nobility inherited their Christianity from their Romano-British ancestors, who would have had little choice but to conform to the late empire's religious and social norms. Of course, that conformity would have ranged from mere token gestures to full adoption of the new faith. We can guess that the more dogmatic elements of the Celtic Church were probably restricted to the upper classes still resident in the old urban centres, while the further one travelled from the places of political power the balance of spiritual power shifted back to the older paganism. According to at least one mediaevel writer, in the Rheged of Taliesin's day, many 'among the mountains were given to idolatry, or ignorant of the Divine law',[52] suggesting Taliesin wasn't always travelling amongst fellow Christians.

Neither are we totally clear what type of Christianity was popular amongst the Welsh nobility. It was certainly a flavour of Roman Catholicism, but early Welsh Christianity also had its own uniquely Celtic perspectives, including several that had been deemed heretical on the continent. What blend of Christian and pagan beliefs was most pervasive is impossible to judge; in the historical Taliesin's poetry, some mention is made of the Christian God, but little else to suggest how much of the native paganism had been adapted to fit the relatively new Christianity.

---

52 Jocelyn of Furness, *Vita Sancti Kentigerni* Ch.23, c. 1200 CE.

After crossing the Ribble, Taliesin would have headed north through the forests and fens, aiming for the ruined Roman fortress of Calunium on the River Lune, present day Lancaster. Lune probably commemorates an original Welsh name that could have been *Llawn*,[53] giving Afon Llawn, 'the abundant river', in Taliesin's time. After crossing the Lune and following the Roman road for a while, the tops of the Lake District would have appeared on the north-western horizon and the more rounded humps of the Yorkshire dales in the north-east. Somewhere between the two ranges, his path left the low forests and started climbing to the moors. At some of the higher points, Ynys Manaw[54] would have appeared on the western horizon, a mysterious island in the Irish sea that was — as far as Taliesin had heard — a real place.

As he left the higher ground, he would have descended into the Eden Vale, a long strip of land surrounded by a long horseshoe of mountains open to the north at present-day Carlisle. To the south-east of what is now the town of Penrith (a Welsh name probably meaning 'Red Hill'), Taliesin would have entered the territory of Llwyfenydd,[55] the home of the king of Rheged, the great Urien. As he approached his final destination, he would have seen a large thatch-roofed hall sat

---

53 Llown; 'own' as in 'brown'.

54 UN-is MAN-ow; 'ow' as in 'sow'. The Isle of Man.

55 Lloo-i-VEN-ith. The area surrounding present day Lyvennet River.

in the middle of a timber stronghold. The place would have been busy with fighters, traders and cow-herders encouraging the lowing beasts into pens. The first official to greet him was probably the *penteulu*,[56] 'the chief of retinue', who oversaw the court's business at home and acted as a first captain in war. The court may well have been forewarned of Taliesin's arrival, the young bard wishing to make as big a splash as possible from the outset. His initial success depended upon impressing his new hosts and assuring them he was a bard of the highest quality and status.

Eight of the twelve historical poems that have come down to us are addressed directly to Urien, and Sir Ifor Williams assumed they could be arranged in some chronological order. Taking for granted that Williams' sequence is correct, the first poem appears to have been composed on the occasion of Urien's successful defence of his northern border at a place called Gwen Ystrad,[57] which either means 'Blessed Vale' or 'Gwên's Vale' (Gwên being a man's name here), specifically at a ford. Rivers created natural boundaries between territories, and battles were often fought at river crossings, so much so that 'the combat at the ford' became a popular motif in many traditional literatures, Welsh bardic poetry being only one of them. The attackers were probably Pictish warriors on

---

56 Pen-TAY-li.

57 Gwen US-trad.

horseback, and Taliesin accompanied Urien and his retinue to bear witness to the fight. Urien was, of course, victorious, or Taliesin's career may well have been cut rather short. On his return with the successful war band, Taliesin may have taken a few days to compose his poem in celebration of Urien's victory.

The warriors of Rheged gather in the thatch-roofed hall where a large hearth fire burns. Urien sits in a prominent position, perhaps on a raised dais. He has long, flowing white hair and beard, and his body is covered with many battle scars. The hall is busy with the chatter and merry-making of his retinue and their families; ale and mead flows and valuable gifts and food are shared amongst the crowd. Taliesin comes to the fire, and everyone grows quiet. He begins his poem with a greeting to the retinue and proclaiming Urien's prowess as a battle leader, victorious raider and scourge of his enemies. Then Taliesin testifies to what has taken place:

> Like waves that cry out grievously over meadows,
>
> I saw hosts of brave men.
>
> And after morning's battle, bruised flesh.
>
> I saw a whole host of dead foreigners.
>
> A lively and fierce shout was heard.
>
> Enduring grief and exhausted soldiers
>
> Were seen as Gwen Ystrad was saved.

> In the gap at the ford, I saw stained men
>
> Dropping their weapons before the grey-haired warrior,
>
> Craving peace. These went as slaves
>
> With their crossed, white hands on the ford's gravel.[58]

This type of poem accomplishes a few things. It shows that Taliesin can perform a basic function for Urien: he is a reliable witness that can confirm the devastating supremacy of his lord. Taliesin saw with his own eyes how the war-chief beat the enemy and defended his territory, proving that he truly was a man worthy of being king. The poem, declaimed publicly before the assembled retinue, would have also been a moment of pride for those fighters, an authoritative witness testifying to their aggression and bravery. They also would have understood that their glorious victory had been laid down in the collective memory, forever preserved in the oral tradition of the ancient bards. Of course, it was the skill with which Taliesin crafted his words, the elegance and artistry of his composition, which ensured the memory was enshrined. A dull reporting of events would not have endured the night, never mind a millennium and a half.

Having proven himself to Urien and his court, Taliesin would have been given patronage for his poem and its

---

58 My translation of the text in Williams (1960), 2.

performance. This confirmed his position and would have been a tacit invitation for him to continue his work. It's possible that Taliesin taught some apprentices this poem in praise of Rheged's king. There may also have been professional declaimers who frequented the court, performers who weren't bards in their own right, but committed to memory important poems and songs that people wanted to hear. In this way, Taliesin's poem may have travelled well beyond Urien's stronghold, becoming part of the oral culture of the region and propaganda for the king.

In another poem to Urien, Taliesin gives more general praise:

Urien of Erechwydd,	most generous man,
You give myriad gifts	to the men of the world.
As you hoard	so you scatter.
The poets of the nations rejoice	for your life's duration.
Joy is made great	by such a famed hero,
Glory made greater	by Urien and his children —
And he a leader,	an exalted chief-king,
Traveller's patron,	first in the battle-horde.
The English know them,	and speak of them:
They had death	and disappointments;
Urien's men burned their lands	and stole their arms.
Frequent losses,	hard suffering

and no relief	from Urien Rheged.
Rheged's defender,	famous lord, nation's anchor,
I favour you	having heard of you.[59]

Although impossible to convey in translation, when reading the original Welsh text, it's clear that Taliesin was a very skilled poet, suggesting the Welsh bardic tradition he was trained in was already ancient in the sixth century. This poem tells us about the relationship between Taliesin and Urien, between bard and king. In the last two lines, *'I favour you / having heard of you'*, Taliesin claims that because of Urien's fame as a great war chief, he has chosen freely to come and praise him. In other words, Taliesin declares he has some independence of opinion, that he can choose who he wants to celebrate. This claim to some kind of objectivity, to truly judge the worthiness of a king and patron, was an important part of how Taliesin presented himself publicly.

In other poems, Taliesin's personality is a little more apparent:

My courage asks — O great labour! —

'Shall I tell you what I see to be true?'

I saw before the lord (he did not see me)

Every favourite boldly giving his message.

---

59 My translation of the text in Williams (1960), 3.

I saw this Easter an abundance of produce,

I saw leaves coming forth, as always,

I saw a branch of unrivalled flowers,

I saw a lord most generous in morals,

I saw the leader of Catraeth over the meadows.

(May he be my prince — others fear him!)

As payment for my song, his gifts will be great,

Chief of men who gifts me a large herd.

My awen is an ash spear,

My shield from the lord is my fresh, bright smile.[60]

Here, Taliesin is comparing his own role as a bard to Urien's role as a warrior. Where Urien has an ash spear and a shield, Taliesin has his awen and a bright smile.

The Taliesin we find in this very early poetry is bold, direct and possesses powerful speech. He has a certain machismo and mystique, two of the key characteristics of his later legendary figure. This historical Taliesin is also proud and full of grace, passionate and bright — again, attributes we can easily find in the legendary bard of later myth and folklore. Taliesin's style influenced Welsh bardic poetry for the next millennium. Ensuing generations of Welsh bards found that

---

60 My translation of the text in Williams (1960), 9.

emulating Taliesin's attitude and personality was conducive to a successful career at court. This was probably a major factor in his ascension to the position of legendary founding father of the bardic tradition.

That the historical Taliesin claims awen as the chief weapon in his bardic arsenal suggests the central role it played in early bardic culture. If the awen of the sixth century was as profound a spiritual power as that of later periods, then it was not an offhand statement by Taliesin; he was showing the king his licence, metaphorically, to practise as a court bard. In later centuries, we see the bards organised into guilds that jealously guarded the poetic craft that gave shape to their awen, a craft that enabled them to produce such elegant and artful verse. They claimed their unique ability to draw on this divine source of inspiration set them apart from common buskers and wandering minstrels, lower-class performers they sought to muscle out of the noble halls lest they take the patronage the bards believed was rightfully theirs.

Taliesin appears to have been dedicated to Urien's cause for some time. But he may also have travelled to other Welsh kingdoms to praise other great war chiefs. Amongst the twelve historical poems to have survived, there are two composed for a Gwallog, probably the ruler of the neighbouring kingdom of Elfed,[61] situated to the south-east of Rheged in present-day

---

61 ELV-ed.

Leeds and Sheffield. The major threats to Elfed came from the kingdoms of Deira to the east and Mercia to the south, Angles and Saxons respectively, but Gwallog appears to have been a significant warlord keeping these dangerous enemies at bay and even forming an alliance with his distant relation Urien and other Welsh kings to take on the increasing power of the Angles. In one poem, Taliesin lists Gwallog's many victories, including:

> A battle by the sea (hearty praise for him!)
>
> Tormenting the men of York.
>
> A battle in Bro Bredrwyn with the heat of great fire,
>
> Stout his hatred.
>
> A battle by the Fortresses of Tegion,
>
> A hundred battalions quaking in Aeron.[62]

The battalions of Aeron would have been Urien's men, said here to be quaking out of fear of the great Gwallog. In the second praise poem, Taliesin recounts how Urien gave hostages to the king of Elfed, implying subservience. In this case, Taliesin's fame and the desire of declaimers to spread his poetry far and wide did not serve the bard well. Urien may have got wind of the glorious praises heaped upon Gwallog, and as a result his own portrayal as a grovelling failure. Being bested by

---

62 My translation of the text in Williams (1960), 13.

his neighbour was not how Urien wished to be remembered. It appears Taliesin was warned of Urien's displeasure and sought to patch things up with a *dadolwch*,[63] a type of poem designed to reconcile the bard with an estranged or offended patron:

The most excellent ruler
I approach Urien,
When I am in anguish,
It is the best of regions
I care little
I won't go to them;
I'll go to the north
Even though I ask for much,
Without needing to boast,
Lands of Llwyfenydd,
Mine their joy,
Mine their garments,
Mead from cups
From the best king,
The kings of all peoples
Before you they moan,
And while I may
There was none better

I'll not abandon:
to him I will sing.
I will find a welcome.
under the chief of rulers.
for the princes I see;
I'll not be with them,
to great kings.
I'd bet a lot more
Urien will not refuse me.
mine their riches,
mine their gains,
mine their luxuries.
and endless goods
most generous with his praise.
are slaves to you.
they must be on their guard.
joke around with the old man,
before I knew him.

---

63   Dad-OL-wch; 'ch' as in 'loch'.

Now I see   how much I receive.

But for God supreme,   I will not renounce him.

Your kingly sons,   most generous of men,

Will sing their songs   in their enemies' lands.

And until I am feeble with age

And in grievous need of death,

I will not be joyful

Unless I praise Urien.[64]

It's unclear if this *dadolwch* was enough to appease the old king. With no way of knowing the actual chronology of these historical poems, we can only guess if Taliesin was truly reconciled with Urien. If so, it's unlikely things were ever the same again. The society in which they lived placed a high price on honour, and to be shamed could be a fate worse than death. Perhaps the old war chief was mature enough to realise a great bard like Taliesin, a poet who appeared to be welcome at the courts of several Welsh kings, could provide a unique service to those who could afford it. Even in the crude terms of propaganda, his praise poems furnished his patrons with a powerful reputation. But perhaps Urien also understood implicitly that the Welsh bards were the only ones who could

---

64 My translation of the text in Williams (1960), 11.

ensure a king's reputation truly survived his death. Only they could enshrine the memory of a mortal man and ensure he was remembered as an immortal hero. Mythologising the nobility in this way was one of the most powerful services they could sell to their patrons.

Especially in times of great violence, such as the period Taliesin and Urien both lived through, the brutal limitations of a warrior's life were ever apparent. To be blessed by awen in a public commemoration, elegantly wrought in the chiming sounds of beautiful bardic poetry, must have seemed like a boon more precious even than the spoils of war. Reputation and fame are amongst the very few things the dead can keep. All of this is implied in the elegy Taliesin composed in commemoration of Urien's son, Owain:

> The soul of Owain ab Urien:
>
> Consider, Lord, its need.
>
> A king beneath Rheged's green kingdom.
>
> It's not hard to sing his praise.
>
> The famed one in a low cell,
>
> His dawn-winged spear burning.
>
> For there is no equal
>
> To bright Llwyfenydd's lord,

Enemy's reaper, firm grip,

Bold as his father, as his grandfather.

When Owain killed Fflamddwyn,[65]

It was no more than sleeping:

Now Lloegr's[66] vast war-band sleep

With light in their eyes.

Those who retreated little

Were braver than was needed.

Owain, in fury, punished them

Like a wolf hunting sheep.

Fine man, his weapons mottled,

Gave horses to those who asked.

Riches like a miser he hoarded.

He shared them for the sake of his soul,

The soul of Owain ab Urien.[67]

Later bards believed this to be the finest elegy ever composed
in the Welsh language. I must admit to feeling like I've mangled
something precious in translating it, but at least it gives the bare

---

65   FLAM-thoo-in.

66   LLOI-gur. The Angles and Saxons.

67   My translation of the text in Williams (1960), 12.

meaning of one of the most famous poems in Welsh literature. In creating such a work, Taliesin kept his promise to ensure the heroic reputation of Urien's son down the ages. Had he not been able to keep that promise, you would not be reading this poem now.

In Taliesin's poems for Urien, there are three prominent characters: Taliesin himself, Urien, and his son Owain, the implication being he was the natural heir to his father's kingdom. It was tragically common that the sons of the warrior elite perished before their fathers, and as we have no elegy for Urien, the end of Owain's life may have marked a slow but sure unwinding of Urien's power. The mercurial Taliesin may have seen the deterioration of the kingdom as inevitable, and left before the collapse accelerated. To quote again from the ninth- century Latin history, *Historia Brittonum*, Urien was finally assassinated by another Welsh king in the year 590 CE:

> . . . *and whilst he was on an expedition, he was murdered, at the instance of Morcant, out of envy, because he possessed so much superiority over all the kings in military science.*

We don't know what happened to Taliesin after leaving Urien's court for the last time. As the wave of Angles and Saxons continued to gnaw away at the Welsh kingdoms of the Old North, Taliesin may have left for the relative safety of present day Mid Wales, perhaps returning home to a more peaceful (but less glorious) career.

Overlooking the Dyfi estuary, where on a clear day the translucent isle of Enlli[68] can be seen shimmering out in the Irish Sea, there is a burial mound that bears the name Bedd Taliesin, 'Taliesin's Grave'. It sits above the small village of Tre Taliesin, 'Taliesin's Town'. It's disputed exactly how old these names are, but they tell us that there is at least a folk memory of this being the last resting place of Taliesin Ben Beirdd, Chief Bard of the West.

---

68   EN-lli.

CHAPTER 3

The Bards

Fair Elffin, stop your weeping;
Hoping for the worst will do no good.
Never was anything better had in Gwyddno's weir
Than [what was found] this evening.

Taliesin could not have achieved all that he did alone. The charged and beautiful poetry that he composed did not leap out of his mouth unprompted, no matter what the folktale claims. The Welsh bardic tradition that fostered him and taught him his craft had its roots in the earlier Brythonic tradition of the ancient Celtic tribes, and was therefore already ancient by Taliesin's time. He could reach such lofty heights of poetic artistry because he was standing on the shoulders of giants, masters of bardic craft whose names are now long forgotten. Not only was Taliesin the fruit of such a great wizened tree, but after his death he was buried in the fertile soil of its roots, and became a part of the living body of bardic lore: the same tradition continued to preserve the best of his work, keeping it alive in the collective imagination of his people. More than that, he was given an honour few others were granted, becoming the spirit of the tradition itself. He was transformed into a legendary hero who spoke with the voice of all the bards that came before and after him.

In practical terms, he was one of the more important symbols for the ancient bardic orders of Wales, a symbolic standard for their training in particular. It was their claim to expert knowledge and skill that made them so valuable to the warrior elite, and they did far more than compose pretty verses. The bardic guilds were led by chief bards who took on various responsibilities at the noble courts, including educating not only their own bardic apprentices but also the young nobility and the heirs of noble houses; they could sometimes act as advocates and some were even trained lawyers; they also functioned as ambassadors and emissaries on behalf of their patrons.

One of the most important roles a chief bard could take on was that of a *pencerdd,* or 'chief of bardic craft', a master of a troop of apprentices. One of the teaching tools a *pencerdd* used was the catalogue of traditional knowledge known as the *trioedd,*[69] or 'triads'. These were maxims or guidelines of bardic craft organised into groups of three, for example:

---

69 TREE-oith.

> *Three things that make a poem strong: depth of meaning,*
> *regularity of Welsh and excellence of imagination.*[70]

Depth of meaning is, of course, a quality of language that's central to the poetic arts; surface ornamentation or narrative is only one part of the craft, the other being what we may call symbolic meaning, a deeper sense that's implied or inferred through metaphors, comparisons, similes, symbols and the like. This depth also evokes the idea of the Welsh otherworld, Annwfn, but more on this later. Regularity of Welsh simply means grammatically correct and technically consistent language; excellence of imagination is obviously a prerequisite in the mastery of any art, here noted as one of the three cornerstones of a good poem. Conversely, another triad tells us:

> *Three things that make a poem weak: vulgar imagination,*
> *shallow meaning and a lack of Welsh.*[71]

Superficial poetry that didn't have depth, or to put it another way, that couldn't express much beyond a literal, surface meaning, was deemed unskilled and unworthy of a court bard. As well as advice for the composition of poetry, there were also guidelines for how it should be performed:

---

70 My translation of the text in G.J. Williams & E.J. Jones (eds.), *Gramadegau'r Penceirddiaid* (UWP 1934), 17.

71 My translation of the text in Williams & Jones (1934), 17.

Three things a poem likes: clear declamation, skilful construction, and the authority of the bard.[72]

How the bards presented themselves publicly during their court performances was of great importance. The mantle of tradition could lend authority, but it was meaningless if the bard simply couldn't perform. No matter how much a bard could make himself look like an ancient druid or wise man, if he was weak of voice and lacked confidence he would fail to do much more than attract the bare minimum of respect. Even if the assembled court acknowledged him a fully signed up member of the old bardic club, he still needed to have presence and style. He certainly wouldn't last long, surrounded as he was by men who practiced far more dangerous and life-threatening arts, war chief amongst them. A Taliesin-like boldness and confidence would have been a necessity in such an environment.

By extension, the bard's reputation was clearly important, and maintaining that reputation while addressing the court publicly was essential:

Three things a poem does not like: feeble declamation, vulgar imagination, and the dishonour of the bard.[73]

---

72   Ibid.

73   My translation of the text in Williams & Jones (1934), 17.

How could a bard lift the spirits of the gathered nobility and direct their gaze to the heroic ideal if he himself was mired in disreputable rumour and gossip? Of course, status could be assumed regardless of reputation, depending on how much raw political power and influence a bard possessed. But too much of a bad smell would surely linger and eventually result in noble patrons turning their noses.

Beyond all else, what confirmed a bard's status and authority was the standard of his craft. Only the greatest of bardic practitioners became bardic masters, and only these masters could attain high office. As a result, a bard's success rested upon a few simple factors:

> *Three things that make awen for a bard: genius, and practice, and art.*

It may sound a little trite when stated in such obvious terms, but what enabled a bard to channel the divine awen was genius (natural ability), consistent practice, and an immersion in the art of bardic poetry itself, the formal craft of the tradition. One would have expected a spiritual power such as awen to need something a bit more mystical to acquire it, but through long experience, the bards knew that its acquisition required nothing more mundane than hard work and a little talent. Inspiration remains a transitory enlightening if you have no practice or craft to give it voice in the world.

The ability to remain consistently productive in one's poetic endeavours was a little more involved. To maintain a long career, there must be a way of ensuring quality throughout one's work. A flash of genius could draw attention, but it was worthless if it fizzled out after a few poems. And so:

> *Three things that make a bard consistent: the telling of tales, and poetry, and the traditional poetry.*[74]

Feeding one's imagination and reflecting upon the broader community of art is a reliable way of remaining consistently inspired. The first piece of advice, the telling of tales, suggests a bard would need to be familiar with the body of traditional narratives, and indeed we find plenty of triads cataloguing the different stories a bard was expected to know.[75] If mediaevel Welsh prose classics are anything to go by,[76] these were often mythologically potent and symbolically intense stories, conveying worldly wisdom and mystic insight, intrigue, adventure and enchantment. Welsh prose classics such as *The Four Branches of the Mabinogi* (eleventh century) or *How Culhwch Won Olwen*[77] (twelfth century) show how such tales

---

74   My translation of the text in Williams & Jones (1934), 18.

75   See Rachel Bromwich, *Trioedd Ynys Prydein* (UWP 2014).

76   See Sioned Davies, *The Mabinogion* (OUP 2007). This is a collection of eleven mediaevel Welsh tales, all written sometime between the eleventh and fourteenth centuries. They are traditional in nature and draw on much older material preserved in the oral myths of ancient Wales.

77   KILL-ooch.

were treasure troves of traditional knowledge in their own right, preserving as they did a distillation of traditional lore.

Of course, the key was the *telling* of such tales, not just the simple remembering of them. When a performer brings such cultural treasures to life in the imaginations of an audience, they are given access to the myth from the inside. As every performer worth their salt knows, sparking imaginations requires a practised imagination of one's own, and if a story is to come alive, it must first live in the heart and soul of its teller. Returning night after night to the internal world of a thoroughly good story gives a tangible sense of its living power. Characters live through you, emotions pour out of you, journeys are taken inside of you to lands you see clearly in your mind's eye. It's the vividness of these subjective experiences for the performer that makes a story so engaging for an audience. The chief bards clearly understood this and appreciated the beneficial effects it could have on a willing apprentice.

The telling of tales was also good practice for the declamation of poetry. Even though both are different types of performance, they both require at least a basic understanding of the dramatic persona and the conveying of genuine emotions. Indeed, just as Taliesin exemplifies in his praise of Urien, the persona of the bard is key to persuading an audience to come along for the ride. Genuine feeling and powerful expression are needed if a performer is to gain an audience's trust, and without that trust, an audience cannot buy into a performance. Particularly during solemn occasions at court, the gravity of the situation could easily result in a cold crowd. Penetrating that frigid atmosphere and warming an audience up requires a projection of one's personality and confidence in one's voice.

The persona adopted by court bards for their public ceremonies of praise and commemoration was one of authority and mystic power. They subtly positioned themselves as a secular priest class, a professional order in possession of great spiritual wisdom and divine inspiration. Not that this was ever explicitly stated, as openly claiming to be a type of priest would have clearly attracted the ire of the official religious order: the mediaevel Church. But even taking on the very public role of mystic celebrant was probably challenging enough to the clergy. There may have been a natural competition between the bardic guild and the Church for access to the powerful men of the court, and even though there is no sign of an overt conflict, there are hints that things were not always harmonious between these two political organisations.

According to some twelfth-century poems, there wasn't much love lost between some court bards and the clergy of the day. These poems were composed by bards working in the voice of the legendary Taliesin, implying they would have performed these poems in the guise of the great bardic master. It appears as if some bards at least found him a suitable character for the haranguing of church-men. For example, the poem 'Prif Gyfarch Gelfydd' ('The First Artful Bidding') begins like this:

> The first artful greeting in verse — where could it be read?
>
> Which comes first: darkness or light?
>
> Where did Adam come from? What day was he created?
>
> What was the foundation of the earth founded upon?
>
> He in Church orders does not want to think seriously;
>
> So many of them are sinners
>
> The people's priests will lose the land of heaven.[78]

These are tough questions that those in orders were deemed too ignorant to answer. Even the monks' Christian learning was thought to be weak, with biblical questions left hanging in challenge. Questions of natural philosophy, about the workings of creation, were also beyond the ken of the clergy:

---

78 My translation of the text in Marged Haycock (ed.), *Legendary Poems from the Book of Taliesin* (CMCS 2015), 54. My translations throughout differ from Haycocks, and even though they are more than sufficient, I also encourage any serious students of Taliesin poetry to refer to Haycock's edition.

Do the bookmen know

Where night-time or tide come from?

Where their end is?

Where the night goes at dawn?

How does it happen without you seeing it?[79]

The implication here is that the oral learning of the bards was superior to the book learning of the clergy, perhaps because the preservation of knowledge in books weakens the mind. The legendary Taliesin also shows off his own mystical abilities, including foretelling the future, something the clergy had no claim to:

They currently enjoy pleasure

But they will join in the great burning,

The Cymry in a state of lamentation;

Souls will be tested

When they face the damned host.

The Cymry the worst of the wretches,

A people who lost God's blessing.[80]

---

79 My translation of the text in Haycock (2015), 56.

80 Ibid.

We don't know who this 'damned host' is, but it was usually the English in this type of prophecy poetry, or sometimes the Vikings or the Irish. Yet even though the poem is critical of the clergy, this doesn't make the legendary Taliesin himself any less of a Christian; much of his prophetic knowledge is actually quite biblical in style and content. He suggests that the downfall of a kingdom can be blamed on the sinfulness of its people. This was an old attitude even in the twelfth century. Welsh churchmen like the sixth-century Gildas had claimed the Welsh were made destitute because of the many faults of their secular and religious leaders; displeasing God so thoroughly caused their misfortunes.

These twelfth-century court bards weren't using the legendary Taliesin to subvert Christian teaching, but to challenge the supremacy of the intellectual culture of the Church and their claim to be teachers of Christian knowledge. It was also challenging them on their own turf, a characteristically bold move by the legendary Taliesin. The Church was one of the most powerful institutions in mediaeval Europe, yet Taliesin, the embodiment of the Welsh bardic tradition, is claiming they are unworthy of that privilege because their knowledge is shallow, not founded upon an ancient tradition of divine inspiration like that of the Welsh bards.

In another poem, the great bard asks the monks, '*Why don't you try to catch me out, / now that you are not pursuing me?*'[81] the suggestion being that at least some amongst the clergy had persecuted the legendary persona adopted by the bards. What we have in this couplet is perhaps an insight into the attitudes of the more dogmatic church, critical of a borderline-heretical guild of Christian poets who claimed to have their own independent connection to God. Awen is a native concept with its origins in the pagan past, and it was an easy target for a clergy wanting to find devilish influences in their main competitors.

Whereas awen was a term used frequently in the bardic poetry of the twelfth century, by the middle of the thirteenth, it had almost totally disappeared from the vocabulary. Although it's not clear why there was such a decline in using the term, one reason could be that the more reactionary elements in the Church had forced the bards to reconsider the more heretical elements of their craft.[82] The term was taken up once again by later bards, but its origin and nature remained problematic to some Christians for centuries to come.

---

81   My translation of the text in Haycock (2015), 242.

82   Y Chwaer Bosco, 'Awen y Cynfeirdd a'r Gogynfeirdd', in *Beridd a Thywysogion* (GPC 1996), 22, edited by Morfydd E. Owen and Brynley F. Roberts.

Sometime in the 1420s, Rhys Goch Eryri,[83] an eminent bard of his age, was considering a response to an old friend of his, Siôn Cent, a Breconshire clergyman who had a rather complicated relationship with the Welsh bardic tradition.[84] Rhys Goch understood perfectly well that, just like him, Siôn Cent had received a bardic education and was versed in the traditional forms of the craft. He could compose verse as well as anyone.

But Siôn Cent was also a bit of a miserable old bugger; he was one of those preachers who was fixated on sin and the sorry state of the world, finding fault everywhere he looked, including in the tradition of bardic poetry. Using his not insubstantial skills, he had composed a powerful bardic satire on the awen of the Welsh bards. It was a scandalous and provocative poem and, as Siôn well knew, there was nothing like a bit of controversy to make people want to hear what all the fuss was about. He had used poetry as a pulpit from which to preach against the professional poets. Rhys Goch Eryri was obliged to respond.

Rhys would probably have first heard the poem given voice by professional declaimers, and may even have seen a written copy of it. Although not the lengthiest of polemics, the main argument was substantial:

---

83   Rees Gawch Air-UR-i; 'aw' as in 'lawn'. c. 1365 - 1440.

84   Shawn Kent. c. 1367 - 1430.

Doubtless, there are two distinct awen

In the bright path of the world:

Christ's awen, joyful matter,

Of the true way, perfect awen,

She was given gracefully

To the prophets and masters of praise,

Holy angels in Seth's Glen

Producing unceasing metre;

The other awen (the unwise sing

Trusting in a dirty lie),

She was given to arrogant men,

To the pretentious bards of the Welsh. . . .

The simple man that loves praise

Believes it like an oath on a relic.

Oh God, who's the most foolish of the two,

The man, or the 'best' of bards? . . .

She's an awen, weak her claim,

From the oven of infernal nature[85]

---

85 My translation of the text in Henry Lewis et al (eds.), *Cywyddau Iolo Goch ac Eraill* (UWP 1937), 181-2.

This was, of course, a direct challenge to the native bardic tradition to which Rhys Goch belonged. It was his vocation to praise the living nobility and commemorate them in death. According to Siôn Cent, the awen Rhys and his fellow bards used to flatter important men was nothing but the muse of hell, a source of falsehoods and deception. Only poetry directed to the glory of God could ever truly be said to be divinely inspired. Even though Sion Cent's poem was probably intended to rile the bards, to provoke them into responding, Rhys Goch couldn't for the life of him keep his tongue. The awen was stirring and wanted to be given voice. He had long argued against such charges, defending the integrity of the divine bardic awen.

Rhys Goch would have composed his response whilst sitting in one of his bardic 'places'. According to the local tradition of his home village of Nanmor,[86] Rhys had a stone chair on the banks of the River Glaslyn.[87] The stone chair has never been found, but it suggests Rhys often found his awen whilst listening to the whispering of the river as it slipped by. Sitting in his special spot, watching the silvered surface of the waters turn, Rhys found the words that would challenge his miserable old friend's charge:

---

86 NAN-mor; 'o' as in 'song'.

87 GLASS-lin.

There are two extraordinary types of awen,

You say, wondrous of kind.

One God given, melody of pure grace,

In the sight of His angels;

And a foul, disharmonious awen,

Lying, deceitful of word,

Whom the bards and poets of the world

have been given, causing agitation.

Know then, you amazingly hardy filth,

(Frail Siôn, clanking like dull brass,

With meter-scaffolded, unworthy text)

There is but one awen.

From the Holy Ghost, worthy praise-song,

It arises to the tongue,

And from heaven, home of every gift,

It is sent often

On condition that God's praise

Is sung well.[88]

---

88   My translation of the text in D.F. Evans (ed.), *Gwaith Rhys Goch Eryri* (UWP 2007), 106.

Rhys Goch's position was simple: there is only one awen and so long as the bards don't neglect to praise God, there isn't a problem. This gave Rhys and his fellow bards a Christian authority that was not under the direct control of the Church. In another poem, he claims that neither great literature nor significantly knowledge of Christ is possible without awen.[89] In other words, a bard's awen was comparable to Scripture! Rhys Goch was confident in the native authority and power of the bardic tradition; it was on equal footing to the clergy and certainly not subservient to it. Although controversial to some in the Church, this wasn't that different to how inspiration was considered elsewhere in European culture. The Holy Spirit was often seen as the source of creativity, an old idea by Rhys Goch's time, and one that had probably been part of the Welsh Christian tradition for long centuries. Of course, clergymen like Siôn Cent believed the Church should have a complete monopoly on all types of divine grace and therefore took action against what they saw as heresy.

It's unclear exactly what Rhys Goch's philosophy was as a Christian, but it appears to include free will. If there is only one awen that's given to all poets, the variety of poetry that issues from it appears to be a matter of personal choice. A poet has the free will to use the divine gift as they wish, for good or ill, and the individual reaps the consequences. Using awen

---

89   Ibid. 8.95–8

for secular purposes, such as praising noblemen, was not a problem so long as it was also used to praise God. The same thinking is often found in the court poetry of earlier bards who would begin their poem by praising God before celebrating the patron. It's even mentioned in the native Welsh laws. This custom may well have been what Rhys Goch was alluding to.

It might be possible to understand the differences between Siôn Cent and Rhys Goch Eryri as arising from different types of Christian philosophy. As a clergyman, Siôn Cent could well have been closer to the Augustinian attitude to free will, that only through God's grace could a sinner be saved. Exercising one's free will and making choices in the world was therefore meaningless. You couldn't choose to be touched by God's grace as that was only in His gift; the choices you made had no impact on whether you would be saved.

Conversely, Rhys Goch's position appears to be closer to that of the old Brythonic heretic Pelagius, a fourth-century British Christian who argued for free will and against predestination. The essence of the Pelagian heresy was the belief that God's grace gave humanity the knowledge of what was good and what was evil, and that people could either abide by that knowledge or ignore it, not that dissimilar to what Rhys Goch's position may have been: that a bard could choose what to do with awen once they had received it. Either way,

Rhys was unwavering in his belief that the bards had received a divine gift unmediated by the Church.

The bardic order's unique access to the divine awen meant it naturally came into conflict with a clergy who claimed a similar power. Rhys Goch Eryri's dispute with Siôn Cent was repeated in later generations, with some poetic disputes between bards and clergymen spanning decades, the same arguments revisited and never resolved.[90] The bards' willingness to fight their corner showed they not only had confidence in their own learning but also in the spiritual foundations upon which their tradition was built. Pressured as they were by successive generations of the clergy, bards such as Rhys Goch would have found it necessary to formulate a coherent defence that accounted for their practice and culture. This often resulted in a hybrid of Christian and pagan philosophy as the bards negotiated a place for their native mythology within their Christian culture.

As a bard's bard, Rhys Goch's poetry was quite typical of the time, following the same slow-moving trends in subject and tone as his contemporaries. It was common to allude to what we may call bardic mythology, or elements of common folklore concerning the bards and their historical craft. In one poem, Rhys Goch dramatises a conversation between himself and two

---

90   See the discourse of Edmwnd Prys and Wiliam Cynwal in G.A. Williams (ed.), *Ymryson Edmwnd Prys a Wiliam Cynwal* (UWP 1986).

mythic forefathers of the bardic tradition, Myrddin[91] and the great Taliesin. He begins the poem by stating:

> The two men of wondrous verse,
>
> I shall not dare to name them,
>
> Adorned as they are in golden sunshine
>
> Beneath the arc of the sun's course.
>
> They pause, winged ones that they are;
>
> It was God who transformed them into men.
>
> It's good to be in the presence of
>
> A man who has wings.[92]

Rhys Goch appears to be saying that he's conversing with Myrddin and Taliesin in the form of birds. There are other poems in the Welsh tradition that describe similarly weird conversations,[93] but in this poem in particular, Rhys may also refer to the fact that both Myrddin and Taliesin were known to have transformed into animals. According to legend, Myrddin was a wild man of the woods who grew hair on his body like a beast, and Taliesin had literally transformed into many animals, one being a bird, in his earlier incarnation as Gwion

---

91 MUR-thin. The the original Welsh character the English Merlin is based upon.

92 My translation of the text in Evans (2007), 116.

93 For example, see 'The Dialogue of Arthur and the Eagle' in N.A. Jones, *Arthur in early Welsh Poetry* (MHRA 2019), 167.

Bach. Rhys also states that it was God who had the power to transform them back into human form. Here he weaves a mixture of different spiritual concepts, ranging from the more pagan transmigration in animal form to the Christian understanding that only the power of God the Creator could perform such miracles. And neither are we mistaking angelic imagery here either, as Rhys Goch himself states clearly:

> One of them dwells
>
> In a place much lower than heaven.
>
> Our two fellows of splendid power,
>
> [One] well-apparelled in Cadair Sidi
>
> And the other, best of careers, rests
>
> Beneath a spring of profound water,
>
> Within the enchanted rock (we praise it)
>
> Of some snowy glen.[94]

Here, Rhys Goch is talking about otherworldly places from Celtic myth, and he positions them in contrast to the Christian heaven. Taliesin is in Cadair Sidi, one name given to Annwfn, the Welsh otherworld, while Myrddin is within an enchanted rock, a reference to his continental counterpart Merlin, being

---

94 My translation of the text in Evans (2007), 116.

imprisoned under a rock for his love of Vivien. In both cases, coupled as they are with the descriptions of the two bards as birds, there is a suggestion that the souls of these ancient masters reside somewhere other than heaven, but neither is it hell. While bards such as Rhys Goch Eryri were Christians, they also adhered to folk beliefs that were clearly pagan in origin. They could describe in imaginative verse how the souls of their bardic masters would talk to them as birds, and they fit this into a Christian understanding of the world. This hybrid culture of Christian and pagan belief exemplifies much of what we find in the Taliesin tradition.

CHAPTER 4

The Spirit of Prophecy

... she meditated upon her arts to see how she could
fill him with the spirit of prophecy and make him
a great storyteller about the world to come.

Ceridwen's ambition for her desperately unpleasant son was that he would become an enlightened bard worthy of high office in the land. In Gruffydd's version at least, it's not a mundane intellect nor bookish knowledge that she seeks for her son, but specifically 'the spirit of prophecy' and the ability to transform that magical insight into stories about the future. Prophecy was a power claimed by the *brudwyr* ('predictors', 'soothsayers'), bards who specialised in prophecy poetry. For them, it was a way of doing politics, as they often sought to influence the outcome of some political struggle or another. They discussed current and future events in heavily coded and symbolic language, usually ambiguous enough to be interpreted in a way favourable to the bard's patrons. As we shall see, for the nobility, paying for a good prophecy poem to be spread about the country at the right time could be politically advantageous.

Elis Gruffydd was very familiar with the Welsh tradition of prophecy and explored the more important prophetic utterances of his age throughout his career. His description of the awen Ceridwen brewed in her cauldron could well have been influenced by the contemporary fascination with Welsh bardic prophecy. Henry VIII's own father, Henry Tudor, had taken the crown of England while riding a wave of popular prophecy that claimed he was *Y Mab Darogan*,[95] 'the Son of Prophecy': a traditional hero who would arise to save the Welsh and take back the British crown for the original inhabitants of the island. Henry Tudor was Welsh on his father's side and could therefore claim to be the mythical son of prophecy.

The figure of *Y Mab Darogan* had been fostered by generations of Welsh bards before Henry Tudor took advantage of it. For centuries, the bards had composed prophetic poems in support of one nobleman or another, each time claiming this or that princeling was the glorious hero destined to lead the Welsh. Some of the great rebels of English-occupied Wales had donned this mythic mantle to bolster their legitimacy as natural leaders, Owain Glyndŵr[96] being perhaps the most famous. Even though his 'prophesied' uprising of 1400 was initially successful, by 1415 it had petered out and the glamour of *Y Mab Darogan* had dissipated, leaving Glyndŵr little more

---

95   Ur Mab Dar-OG-an; in Mab 'a' as in 'hard'.

96   Glin-DOOR.

than a failed hope. But the myth, at least, was kept alive by the Welsh bards, and by the time it was hung around the young shoulders of Henry Tudor, it had been fully restored to its original glory. In the summer of 1485 Henry took the 'bardic road to Bosworth',[97] travelling through Wales on his way to do battle with Richard III, gathering not only material support and troops from amongst his Welsh relations, but also wrapping himself in the ancient mystique of prophecy that only the Welsh bards could give him.

On his way to do battle at Bosworth, Henry passed through the tiny hamlet of Mathafarn[98] in Mid Wales. This was not by accident, for Mathafarn Hall was the home of none other than Dafydd Llwyd, a famous *brudiwr*, a prophecy poet of his time. If Henry could get Dafydd Llwyd to declare that he was truly *Y Mab Darogan*, he could win widespread support amongst the Welsh, particularly the common folk who had suffered long under the harsh apartheid of the English state. Just like the spin doctors of today, by playing on the hopes and fears of ordinary people, a bard like Dafydd Llwyd could convince many to fight for Henry Tudor, a man with whom they had very little in common.

---

97   See G. Williams, 'The bardic road to Bosworth: a Welsh view of Henry Tudor' in *Transactions of the Honourable Society of Cymmrodorion*, 1986.

98   Math-AV-arn.

According to local tradition, Henry Tudor spent the night with Dafydd and his wife. After a lovely dinner and fine conversation, in the middle of his pudding, Henry turned to the bard and asked, 'So, Dafydd. You're a prophecy poet. Can you tell me who's going to win in the great battle of Bosworth? Will it be me, or that dastardly Richard III?'

Taken aback, Dafydd answered uncertainly. 'Well . . . I . . . now then . . . the best thing for me to do is . . . erm . . . to meditate upon this important matter this evening, and I'll give you my answer in the morning . . . ?'

'Fine,' said Henry, and off he went to bed. That night, Dafydd Llwyd couldn't sleep a wink, and was pacing up and down his bedroom keeping his wife awake.

'Dafydd, come to bed!' she cried out.

'Come to bed, woman! Come to bed! How can I sleep knowing I have this prophecy to deliver by morning? If I get this wrong, Henry will have my head!'

To which his wife replied, 'Listen, Dafydd, you have nothing to worry about. If you tell him he's going to win, but he ends up losing *his* head, he will not be in any position to come and take *yours*, will he? You risk nothing by telling him he'll be the victor.'

Dafydd kissed his wife gratefully and slept peacefully until the morning, where, upon waking and greeting the young nobleman over breakfast, Dafydd declared confidently that

Henry was sure to win the day against Richard III. Which, of course, he did.[99]

Dafydd Llwyd composed several prophecy poems to support Henry Tudor's campaign, one in particular that was declaimed before the Welsh troops just before they dashed off into battle to die on behalf of the young aristocrat. It's a remarkable piece of public performance, a rousing call and response between the bard and the troops. The poem also stresses the desperate desire for freedom that many of the Welsh folk would have felt.

Henry Tudor's victory at Bosworth brought an end to several decades of conflict between the houses of York and Lancaster, and was the final chapter in the Wars of the Roses. It also brought an end to an ancient tradition of prophecy, and even though he was the first Welshman to sit upon the English throne, in reality, Henry VII did very little to improve the lot of the Welsh. He was not to be their saviour; if anything, their lives would only get worse as his heir, Henry VIII, took the throne. The bardic propaganda that had been marshalled in support of Henry Tudor's campaign turned out to be a lie. A so-called Welshman may have sat upon the English throne, but the Welsh were as destitute as ever.

---

99 With many thanks to my good friend Owen Shiers for performing this sketch with me on stage countless times.

The myth of *Y Mab Darogan* had genuine power because the Welsh bards were held in such high regard in Welsh society. They had spent countless generations fostering a particular mystique which time and again they put in service of the nobility, for better or worse. Ceridwen wanted her son, Morfran to join their ranks because their traditional, priest-like role gave them direct access to the highest levels of power. Since time immemorial, bards had been officers of the king's court and received patronage for their service. Typically, patronage was given for the composition of praise poetry performed publicly by the bard before the gathered court. If the praise poetry we have in manuscript is anything to go by, these were ceremonial events with some pomp and pageantry.

This celebration of the heroic ideal and the glorifying of the warrior elite was the perfect setting for myths such as *Y Mab Darogan*. The public adoration of the king as a mythical hero, performed with grand ceremony by a chief bard versed in the ancient mysteries of awen, was one of the most effective ways the upper classes had of impressing upon everyone else how important they were. Bardic poetry was the exercise of a mighty cultural power. According to bardic myth, as we have seen, that power had its source in the divine awen, first possessed by a young boy called Gwion Bach who, through the magical enlightenment it conferred upon him, became the mighty Taliesin.

Amongst other things, the legendary Taliesin was regarded a prophet, and many poems foretelling the future were composed in his voice over several centuries. The other famous prophet in the Welsh tradition was, of course, Myrddin, and both he and Taliesin were often mentioned together as paragons of bardic mysticism. One eleventh-century poem recounts a dialogue between the two sages, where they appear to shift from discussing past battles to those of the future, ranging through time in a prophetic dialogue that's both ambiguous yet very traditional in style.[100] The poets appear to be observing time from the outside, taking up a perspective on different periods and comparing them.

It's this same transcendent quality that's often evoked in other poems of the genre, where the vision of the bard encompasses different episodes in the mythical past. But this also has the effect of making the different episodes seem disjointed. In one long series of visions, Taliesin says such things as:

> The Britons will get
>
> Blood of splendid combat;

---

100   A.O.H. Jarman (ed.), *Ymddiddan Myrddin a Thaliesin* (UWP 1967).

After gold and trinkets

Anglesey and Llŷn laid waste,

And refuge in Eryri.

…

A perfect one prophesies

Settlement in wasteland.

The Cymry, perfect language,

Will change how they speak.

There will be the Speckled Cow

To wreak vengeance.

It will bellow at mid-day,

It will plot at midnight,

The farm land will be in turmoil,

Our consecrated places will be destroyed.[101]

Although the prophecy poems attributed to Taliesin were deemed important enough to be recorded in manuscript, by today they can be difficult to enjoy as poetry. That said, some of the imagery is striking, and once again reveals a hybrid mysticism that draws on both Christian and pagan imagery. A

---

101 My translation of the text in Marged Haycock (ed.), *Prophecies from the Book of Taliesin* (CMCS 2013), 128.

particularly bemusing sequence can be found at the beginning of a late thirteenth-century Taliesin prophecy, 'Daronwy':

> God protected Noah
>
> From the Flood, a radiant expanse,
>
> Swiftest to spread out,
>
> Attacking beyond the surging sea.
>
> What tree is greater
>
> Than Daronwy?
>
> He will shelter those
>
> Around Noah's Ark.
>
> There is a greater secret —
>
> Dawn-radiance of Goronwy's men;
>
> A rare man knows it.
>
> Mathonwy's magic wand,
>
> When it grows in the trees,
>
> Promotes abundance
>
> On the bank of the Gwyllionwy.[102]

It's appropriate to begin such a poem by referring to perhaps the most famous prophet in the Christian tradition, Noah. His

---

102   My translation of the text in Haycock (2013), 29.

story is not only proof that God speaks to humanity through prophets, but does so to warn them against coming disaster, perhaps the best reason we should apparently pay attention to the crazy ramblings of this legendary bard. But then we have our first bit of intentional ambiguity, where a great tree by the name of Daronwy appears to be connected to Noah's ark. Are we to identify Daronwy with the ark? Daronwy can at least be understood as meaning 'Goronwy's Oak', implying it belongs to someone important, but who is Goronwy? The editor of the poem, Marged Haycock, suggests the imagery also evokes the image of the Tree of Life and Christ's Cross, but the poem makes no explicit references. The tree is meant to be a mystery.

Just to confound us a little more, the poem claims that the radiance of Goronwy's men is a great secret. Is this referring to a spiritual radiance, a light like a halo, perhaps? Or is this radiance a metaphor for wisdom or knowledge, perhaps the light of divine awen? Does Goronwy's Oak have anything to do with the radiance of Goronwy's men? Again, there are no obvious answers. Drawing us further into the mystery, the next section appears to describe a magic wand that grows on the banks of the Gwyllionwy river, probably an imaginary place as we know of no river by that name. Here, we find a very interesting image that appears to evoke both biblical and native imagery. Wooden staffs that continue to grow through divine power can be found in the Old Testament. In Numbers 17:8 we hear that:

> *... Moses went into the tabernacle of witness; and, behold,*
> *the rod of Aaron for the house of Levi was budded, and*
> *brought forth buds, and bloomed blossoms, and yielded*
> *almonds.*

But in Taliesin's prophecy, the rod is called '*hutlath fathonwy*', literally Mathonwy's magic wand, a name that connects it with one of the mediaevel Welsh prose classics of *The Mabinogion*. In *The Fourth Branch of the Mabinogi* we hear how the king of Gwynedd, Math son of Mathonwy, has a magic wand that's used to transform men into animals and magically bring about the full term of a pregnancy,[103] both episodes suggesting that its power is that of the life force, the power of birth and regeneration.

Once again, a Welsh bard combines the more pagan elements of their culture with that of their Christianity, finding comparable images and similar themes as material for mystical poetry. The ability to wield both native and biblical knowledge was, of course, one of Taliesin's chief claims to supremacy over the clergy. It also protects the more heretical elements of bardic belief against Christian persecution.

From the modern perspective, this poetry can read like well written mumbo-jumbo. Without a bardic order continually promoting its power and authority through the mystique of figures such as Taliesin or Myrddin, there is little reason for

---

103   See Davies (2007), 52-4.

contemporary audiences to pay much attention to it. Yet despite its weirdness, or perhaps because of it, mediaeval audiences were clearly drawn to the warnings implied in these poems. They were marked out as important in the manuscripts in which they were recorded and given some salience by naming actual places as the sites of terrible events to come.[104] In 'Glaswawd Taliesin' ('The Vigorous Song of Taliesin') the bard specifically mentions locations in Gwynedd, in north-west Wales:

> In May, on the [River] Menai, there will be carnage,
>
> On the [River] Conwy there will be more
>
> That will wreak vengeance.
>
> Chilling the death which hastens — ready reward —
>
> From savage iron, an immense blow.[105]

Having heard a popular prophecy such as this, a bondsman living on the shores of the Menai sometime in the late twelfth century may have had second thoughts about crossing the river in May. He certainly wouldn't have wanted to cross the River Conwy in the same month; that would have been asking for trouble. Death and destruction arriving on large boats wasn't as common an occurrence in the north-west of Wales as it was

---

104   There appears to be a bardic scoring system associated with some mediaevel poems, and some of the prophecies have relatively high scores. See Haycock (2015), 257-8.

105   My translation of the text in Haycock (2013), 45.

elsewhere in Britain, but it wasn't unheard of. The reality of such dangers may not have been so apparent to twelfth-century Welsh folk as it was to those who lived through the Viking raids of the ninth, but it was still a real danger. The last Viking raid on Môn wasn't until 1209 CE, when six ships landed and utterly destroyed the town of Llanfaes. This type of prophecy had great appeal because even though it was heavily encoded in mysterious symbols and allusions, it also drew on the real, lived experiences of people. The dangers foretold were recognisable because people remembered them actually happening in the past.

The effect of this type of prophecy was amplified when it came from the mouth of the great Taliesin, Chief Bard of the West, and pure embodiment of the bardic spirit. Later bards clearly used him as a convenient persona to lend credence to their own prophetic musings. And it wasn't just Taliesin who was being employed in this way, but the complete package of his myth. The greatest prophecies were given by the greatest bard because he naturally had the greatest awen and therefore the greatest connection to the divine source. The exact mechanics of how awen delivered prophecy to the mouth of the bard is hardly ever described, but in one Taliesin prophecy, we have some inkling as to how exactly the future was foretold:

The druid foretells

What has been and what will be of avail.

The cloud which scuds over the high ground:

It is the poet who interprets it

[And] will lament like a torrent

On the slopes of the mountain.[106]

In the first line, Taliesin is of course referring to himself as a druid (*derwydd*),[107] and even if we don't know exactly what histories the mediaevel bards told themselves about the Iron Age druids, they certainly saw them as their spiritual ancestors. It may have been part of their common lore regarding druids that they based their prophecies on natural phenomena, such as the movements of birds or animals. It's not known if they considered all natural phenomena as a potential source of knowledge about the future, but in this passage at least, Taliesin the druid interprets the movement of cloud over high ground, and having seen in it a sign of great tragedy, he laments profusely.

This suggests awen needed to be stimulated before it would confer the blessing of prophecy. Creative engagement by the bard was required before awen could flow, and musing upon natural phenomena such as the movement of clouds appears to

---

106   My translation of the text in Haycock (2013), 127-8.

107   DARE-with.

have been the perfect creative stimulus. Of course, reading tea-leaves is pretty much the same type of practice, as is reading the flights of birds. It's not that surprising to find this very common type of prophecy was understood by the Welsh bards.

The underlying concept is that divine creation is ordered according to laws that manifested as patterns in the phenomenal world. Those with a practiced sensitivity to how the divine plan was unfolding, could interpret patterns, reading how creation progressed. The entire philosophy rests on a particular concept of time best illustrated in the Welsh word *eiliad*. The common meaning to this day is 'one moment' or 'one second'. But originally it also meant 'one weave' or one bend in a hurdle's lath. The resulting image is of each moment in time being one weave in creation, like a great Celtic knot-work whose woven patterns can be predicted into the future. But the concept also applies to the creation of poetry: the related verb *eilio*, 'to weave', was often used for the composition of verse, *eilio cerdd* meaning simply 'to weave a poem'. Sometimes performed to the beating of a staff, the regular beats of a poem marked out the regular moments of divine creation as it unfolded. As the inspired bard chanted sacred poetry, he revealed the hidden weaving of time.

CHAPTER 5

Awen

awen *feminine singular noun: poetic inspiration,*
muse, poetic genius or gift.[108]

Awen is a very old concept. The word appears to be of ancient
Celtic origin, perhaps from the Proto-Celtic language
spoken about 3000 years ago. At that time, the word may have
sounded more like *awek*,[109] a noun meaning inspiration or
insight. It appears to belong to an ancient complex of meanings
in the Indo-European tradition that includes the Old Irish
word *aí*, 'poetic art', the Welsh words *awel*, 'breeze', and *anadl*
'breath'.[110] Awen also suggests the feminine noun *gwen*, which
isn't usually considered part of its etymology but could easily
be inferred by a native speaker, particularly someone with a
specialised knowledge of the language such as a bard. *Gwen*

---

108 *University of Wales Dictionary.*

109 See Ranko Matasovic, *Etymological Dictionary of Proto-Celtic* (Brill 2009), 47.

110 Calvert Watkins, 'Indo-European Metrics and Archaic Irish Verse', *Selected Writings* Vol.
2 (Innsbruck 1994), 370-1.

is the feminine form of 'white' and also has the connected meaning of 'blessed', as in *gwynfyd*, literally 'blessed world', the Welsh word for paradise. Taken together, the meaning suggested is a type of blessed breath coming into the bard from a divine source.

This is very similar to the modern English 'inspiration', which literally means 'to be breathed into'. It's derived from the Latin *spiritus* (which also gives the modern English 'spirit') and was understood to mean both 'spirit' and 'breathing'. The Latin culture of the Romans shared many common elements with Greek culture, and some of the earliest texts in the classical tradition echo the same idea, suggesting the connection between inspiration, breath and divinity is very old in Europe. Over 2500 years ago, the Greek poet Hesiod claimed that while he was shepherding lambs the Muses, the Greek goddesses of inspiration and daughters of Mnemosyne ('Memory') . . .

> *. . . breathed into me a divine voice to celebrate things that shall be and things there were aforetime; and they bade me sing of the race of the blessed gods that are eternally, but ever to sing of themselves both first and last.*[111]

This could easily have been said of the mediaevel Welsh bards and their Christian God. In very simple terms, awen was the basis of mediaevel bardic power. Historically, bards such as

---

111   H.G. Evelyn-White (trans.), *Hesiod, Homeric Hymns, Epic Cycle, Homerica* (London 1914), 'Theogony' [29].

Taliesin would have had both political and cultural influence, taking advantage of their direct access to the nobility and acting as their advocates in the public sphere. But to gain such an influential position, Taliesin had to first show that he could draw on and use the spiritual awen; without it, he could never ascend to a status where those more mundane powers were available to him. This reality is expressed rather elegantly in Taliesin's folktale, where the young bard illustrates how awen is the basis of his bardic power.

After his discovery by Elffin in a fish weir, the infant Taliesin goes to live with his new patron and his wife, growing into a young boy overflowing with bardic gifts. As a nobleman, Elffin was expected to attend the court of his king, Maelgwn, for special celebrations such as Christmas. While at Maelgwn's court, Elffin gets himself in trouble . . .

Taliesin Releases Elffin[112]

During the celebrations at court, everyone was praising King Maelgwn for his qualities and for the qualities and chastity of his wife. Then Elffin happened to say: 'Truly, no one can compete with a king but another king. But I would say that I have a wife who is just as chaste as any lady in this kingdom. I

---

112   My translation and adaptation of the text in Ford (1992). This is a slightly shortened version of Elis Gruffydd's original.

also have a bard who is more knowledgeable than all the king's bards.'

Some courtiers told the king about Elffin's boasting, and the king ordered him to be locked up until he had proof of the chastity of his wife and the superiority of his bard. Elffin was put in a great tower of the castle with a large shackle about his feet. The king sent his son, Rhun, to test the chastity of Elffin's wife. Rhun was one of the most wanton men in the world, and no wife nor maid, however irreproachable, could resist him if he had but a moment to talk to her.

As Rhun hastened to Elffin's manor full of resolve to defile his wife, Taliesin told her how the king had put her husband in prison, and that Rhun was coming swiftly, intending to despoil her chastity. So he made the noblewoman dress one of the kitchen girls in her clothes and insisted that the girl's hands were covered with the best rings that she and her husband had in their possession, including his signet ring, which had been sent in advance. Then Taliesin had the maid sit for supper in her mistress' room, and Taliesin made her look like her mistress and the mistress look like the maid.

And as they were sitting prettily for supper, Rhun appeared suddenly at Elffin's manor; he was received joyfully, as all the servants recognised him. And hurriedly they took him to the room where the maid was disguised as the mistress and she arose to greet him happily. And then she sat to her supper a second time and Rhun with her, who joked with the maid with lusty words, she who was playing the part of her mistress. And Rhun put a powder in the maid's drink that made her sleep soundly, and she didn't feel him cutting her little finger off her hand, upon which was Elffin's signet ring. And in this way he did as he pleased with the girl, and then he took the finger and the ring upon it as proof for the king he had despoiled her chastity.

The king was happy when he heard this. As a result, he sent for his council, and he told them all that had happened, and bade Elffin be brought from the prison to be rebuked for his boast. And with that, he said to Elffin: 'Understand that it is nothing but foolishness for a husband to believe his wife regarding the fidelity of her body when he is not with her. Your wife broke her wedding vows last night for sure: see here her finger and your signet ring upon it as proof Rhun slept with her and cut it from her hand while she was asleep. There is no way you can deny she broke her chastity.'

And with that Elffin said: 'With your permission, honoured king, it is true I cannot deny this is my ring as everyone recognises it. But I strongly deny the finger this ring is upon was ever on my wife's hand; the hand this finger was cut from has kneaded rye dough within three days of it being cut, and I can confirm that my wife has not kneaded rye dough since she became my wife.' And the king was indignant at

Elffin's assertion about his wife's chastity, and so he ordered Elffin back to prison a second time, telling him he would not be released until he proved his boast was true, for the skilfulness of his bard as much as for the chastity of his wife.

Throughout all this, Taliesin and Elffin's wife were at Elffin's manor, and Taliesin explained to his mistress how Elffin was in prison because of them. But he bade his mistress be happy by telling her how he would go to Maelgwn's court to release his master. And he took his leave of his mistress and came eventually to the court of Maelgwn, who, with kingly grace, was on his way to his hall for dinner, as was the custom of kings and princes during every important celebration. As soon as Taliesin came into the hall, he saw a place to sit in a quiet corner beside where the bards and performers came to do their duty to the king, as it is customary in the courts for there to be frequent announcements at the important festivals.

The time came for the bards and heralds to proclaim the largess and power of the king and his strength. They came past the place where Taliesin was crouching in a corner behind them, and he stuck out his lip and played *blerwm blerwm* on it with his finger. Those that walked past paid little heed but continued until they came before the king and bowed before him as was required of them, and without saying a single word they stuck out their lips and mocked the king by playing *blerwm* with their fingers as they had seen the boy do earlier.

The sight took the king aback; he was shocked to think that they must all be drunk. As a result, he ordered one lord waiting at his table to tell them to remember where they were, to think of the place they were standing and what they ought to be doing. This the lord did gladly, but it did not cause them to stop their foolishness any sooner. And so a second and third time he sent the lord to tell them to leave the hall. And in the end, the king called on one squire to strike the one called Heinin, the chief bard of the court, on the head. And the squire took a bowl and struck him on the head until he fell on his arse, and he got on his knees and begged the king's leave to show him they were neither stupid nor drunk, but behaved as they did because of the power of some spirit that was in the hall. Heinin said: 'Oh honourable king, let it be known to your grace that it was not because of drunkenness that we cannot speak properly, but because of the power of the spirit that is sitting in that corner in the body of a child.'

The king ordered his squire to fetch the child, and he went to the corner where Taliesin was sitting and brought him before the king, who asked him what he was and from where he had come. Taliesin answered the king in song:

A common chief bard

Am I to Elffin.

And my homeland

Is the land of the cherubim.[113]

And then the king asked him what manner of thing he was, and he answered the king like this:

Johannes the wizard

Called me Myrddin,

But now every king

Calls me Taliesin.

And then the king asked him where he had been, and he told his story to the king:

I was with my Lord

In the heights

When Lucifer fell

to the depths of Hell.

I led with a standard

Before Alexander.

And I know the names of the stars

From north to south.

---

113 Heaven.

I was in Gwydion's Fort,

In Tetragramatton;

I was in Canaan

When Absalom was killed;

I brought seeds

To the Vale of Hebron.

I was in the court of noblemen

Before the birth of Gwydion;

I was a patriarch

To Eli and Enoch.

I was chief keeper

Of the works of Nimrod tower;

I was upon the cross

Of God's compassionate Son.

I was for three periods

In the prison of Arianrhod;

I was in the Ark

With Noah and Alpha;

And I saw the destruction

Of Sodom and Gomorrah;

I was in Africa

Before the building of Rome;

I came here

To the remains of Troy;

And I was with my Lord

In the manger of the oxen and the ass;

I helped Moses

Through the water of the Jordan;

I was in the sky

With Mary Magdalen;

I received awen

From Ceridwen's cauldron;

I was a harp bard

To Lleon the Viking;

I was in the blessed hill

In the court of Cynfelyn,

In a shackle and chain

For a year and a day;

I was made manifest

In the land of the Trinity;

And I am the teacher

Of the entire universe;

And until judgement day, I will be

Upon the face of the Earth;

And it will not be known what my flesh is —

Either meat or fish;

And I was well-nigh nine months

In the womb of Ceridwen the witch;

Previously I was Gwion Bach,

But now I am Taliesin.

And this poem greatly surprised the king and his family. Taliesin declaimed this next poem to show the king and his people the reason for his coming and what he wanted:

Contentious poets, I am competing;

I cannot restrain myself;

I speak prophecy

To those who will hear me;

I am seeking

What I have lost:

To release Elffin from punishment,

From the fort of Deganwy.

And from my lord I will lift

Fetter and chain.

By means of the poem of Deganwy Fort.

Beautiful my excess,

300 poems and more

Is the value of the poem I declaim.

Neither spear will be held,

Nor stone, nor ring,

Nor into my circle

Will come a bard who does not recognise me.

Elffin son of Gwyddno,

Because of an indiscreet remark,

Is under thirteen locks

For praising his teacher.

And I am Taliesin,

Chief bard of the West,

Releasing Elffin

From the resplendent fetter.

After this, Taliesin declaimed a poem for patronage. Then it is said a storm of wind arose until the king and the people were afraid the castle would fall upon their heads. As a result, the king hastily fetched Elffin from the prison and set him before Taliesin. In that time and place, it is said Taliesin declaimed a poem that released the shackle about Elffin's feet.[114]

The gusting of magical wind is found in many folktales, as is the ability to hear whatever is spoken on the wind.[115] But specifically in Celtic culture it's connected to bardic power, as we find in the Irish story of Aí. The king of Ireland was eating a meal when a gust of wind came upon him. The king asked his druid what the wind foretold. 'A child to be born to your brother,' said the druid, 'and his rank will be the same as your own.' Immediately, a boy was born in the house and the king seeks to kill him lest his own status be challenged. But the new-born boy causes all to pause in wonder as he begins to speak, calling for the king to give him the various gifts that are due someone of his station. The druid then names the child Aí son of Ollam.[116] As explained at the very beginning of this

---

114   There are several difficult and ambiguous references in this text, particularly in the poetry, that I will return to later.

115   This is one of the abilities of Math the wizard-king in *The Fourth Branch of the Mabinogi*. See Davies (2007), 47.

116   John Carey (trans.), 'The First Utterance of Aí son of Ollam', in *The Celtic Heroic Age* edited by John T. Koch (CSP 2013), 222.

chapter, *ai* is an old Irish word connected to the Welsh awen and meaning 'poetry' or 'poetic art'; *ollam* (or *ollamh* in modern Irish) was a 'professional poet' or more generally a master and teacher of literature, literally meaning a 'professor' today.

In both of these stories the central image is a magical wind, and in both cases this is a metaphor for how a young bard (infant or teenager) can disrupt the power of kings. Both awen and *ai* are forces which are invisible to the naked eye, yet their powerful effects can be seen in the world, particularly in the realm of secular power. The presence of such similar stories in both the Welsh and Irish traditions suggests that in both societies there were bards that could challenge the very power of kings.

A storm of wind is a very appropriate image for how Taliesin reveals his power at court. It was summoned by the young bard as he described in mystic verse the many lives he had lived, suggesting the very memory of his different incarnations carried a significant power. The human imagination has always found such symbolic images satisfying, seeing one thing (powerful awen) expressed through the form of another (a storm of wind). Like all poets, the Welsh bards were captivated by the ability of words to convey more than just a surface meaning, where 'a storm of wind' means more than just a freak weather event. For them, this joy in the depth of meaning found its fullest expression in the technique of *dyfalu*, 'guessing', where the poet describes something with a run of unexpected metaphors. It can be thought of as a type of riddling, a cornerstone of the poet's art that makes use of the imagination's ability to see one thing as another, to see the wind as supernatural force, fire as love's passion, mortal kings as ideal heroes or plain old bards as mystic druids.

'Kanu y Gwynt' ('The Song of the Wind') is one of the earliest *dyfalu* poems to have survived, and may have been composed sometime towards the end of the twelfth century. It's traditionally connected with our legendary bard, recorded as it is in *The Book of Taliesin*, and mediaevel audiences would have watched it being performed by a declaimer or bard playing the part of the legendary Taliesin, perhaps during a theatrical retelling of the precocious young bard's visit to Maelgwn's court:

> Guess who it is:
>
> Created before the Flood,
>
> A hardy creature,
>
> Without flesh, without bone,
>
> Without veins, without blood,
>
> Without head and without feet.
>
> Not older nor younger
>
> Than he was at the beginning.

He won't turn from his intentions

Through fear or death.

The needs of creatures

He does not have.

Good God, so lively

When he comes at first.

Great is the wealth

Of his Creator.

On the field, in the trees,

With no hand nor foot;

With no feebleness or age,

And no hurt can worry him.[117]

On the surface of it, 'The Song of the Wind' appears to be a simple riddle about the wind, never named yet always implied throughout the different images. But appearances can be deceptive, and just as Gwion Bach transforms in the folktale, the more we consider the poem, the further it transforms into something else.

As we see in several poems in *The Book of Taliesin*, the wizard-bard is always ready to boast of his magical

---

enlightenment, one of his chief claims being that he has direct knowledge of the mysterious awen. In the long poem 'Angar Kyfundawt' ('The Hostile Confederacy'), copied some pages before 'The Song of the Wind' in his *Book*, we find several sections where Taliesin mentions this special knowledge:

> How does the sky's wind
>
> distribute itself?
>
> Why is the mind so lively?
>
> Why so fair?
>
> . . .
>
> Who made poems?
>
> Poems, who made them?
>
> Who pondered meaning?
>
> In books it's been pondered
>
> How many winds, how many waters,
>
> How many waters, how many winds, . . . [118]

From a poet's perspective, a lively mind is inspired, and Taliesin compares such a lively mind with the movements of the wind in the sky. In the later section, both winds and waters appear to be metaphors for awen: elemental and powerful forces moving

---

118   Ibid. 115-6.

in the world. This same idea is echoed in the sixteenth-century folktale, where the young bard calls up a storm of wind by declaiming his poems.

This suggests that 'The Song of the Wind' is not only a riddle about the wind, but could also be a double riddle about awen. It's quite a clever poem, requiring a moment of inspiration to understand that a deeper answer to the riddle is itself inspiration. In more ways than one, 'The Song of the Wind' is an evocation of awen, summoning it to gust through the audience while being celebrated in a marvellous riddle.

As we shall see, many of the legendary poems in *The Book of Taliesin* are a call to the imagination, where appearances transform while essences remain eternal. But for all of their dazzling imagery, for all of their mysterious symbolism and kaleidoscopic effect, these poems never spell out anything certain, leaving the audience to discern for themselves if there is any meaning to be found, if this is a riddle about the wind or whether it also describes awen. That is, after all, the special talent of the imagination: to discover a pattern and give it meaning, to see faces in the trees and magnificent beasts in the clouds, to decipher symbols and interpret the deeper meaning of a story.

But the imagination is an insubstantial beast, a grey mare made of little more than breath. We may ride her to the ends of the Earth, but she vanishes the minute we look at her too closely. That intangible nature has led some to mistrust the imagination's ability to grasp any kind of truth. Compared to the transparency of science or the rigour of philosophy, she seems a rather fickle beast.

But a horse is still a horse, and 800 years ago, when the legendary poems in *The Book of Taliesin* were being performed at court, the intangible nature of the imagination didn't seem to concern the Welsh bards. In fact, they appear to have had a great love for it, revelling in ambiguity, riddles and half-glimpsed meanings, playing with all those ways words can move the imagination and cause awen to gust and blow.

Like most of the other poems in the fourteenth-century *Book of Taliesin*, we don't know who composed 'The Song of the Wind'. Even those poems that are assumed to be the work of the historical Taliesin are at best later versions of lost originals. But one quite intriguing fact was revealed by Marged Haycock in her long decades of research on the ancient *Book*: some of the legendary poems, 'The Song of the Wind' amongst them, can be connected to a late twelfth-century court bard by the name of Llywarch ap Llywelyn.[119]

---

119 LLUH-warch ap Lluh-WEL-in. Also known as Prydydd y Moch, 'The Bard of the Pigs'. See Haycock (2007), 30.

Haycock's research doesn't prove that these poems were composed by him, but the similarity between them and Llywarch's formal court poetry has some implications: either Llywarch ap Llywelyn 1) had unique access to these traditional poems and therefore he alone borrowed phrases and words from them; 2) he reworked these traditional Taliesin poems and, in doing so, left his unique mark upon them; 3) he was the author of these poems. There are at least 16 legendary poems connected to Llywarch ap Llywelyn, so it could be a combination of all three, but the truth of the matter is probably somewhere between the second and third possibilities.

There were probably many poems and stories circulating about Taliesin in Welsh folk culture, so it may not have been difficult for Llywarch to find older texts that he could rework. For sake of argument, I'm assuming that Llywarch did most of this work sometime towards the end of the twelfth century, but it could easily have been a project he returned to throughout his long career, which began in 1175 and ended around 1220. This is no small claim. Llywarch ap Llywelyn was one of the highest ranking court bards of his day, and the fact he's connected to these legendary poems tells us a great deal about the role Taliesin's myth played at the highest levels of Welsh society.

Twelfth-century Wales was a different place to that of the sixth century. The Old North, those ancient Welsh kingdoms that had once stretched from the midlands all the way up western England and into the Scottish borders, had disappeared some centuries before. Rheged had been united with Northumbria through marriage not long after Urien's death and the remaining Welsh kingdoms (except Strathclyde) had been taken by the Anglo-Saxons by the early ninth century. Poorer Welsh natives would have stayed, slowly but surely adopting the language and culture of their new Germanic lords, while those that could would have fled to the safety of the surviving Welsh kingdoms in present-day Wales. The refugees would have brought with them their own culture and history, including Taliesin's original poetry, which is why the Old North has such a substantial presence in early Welsh literature.

The memory of these lost kingdoms lived on in the ever-youthful golden age which persisted in the Welsh imagination, its heroes and legends becoming those of the western kingdoms. It's worth stressing that the three founding fathers of the mediaevel Welsh bardic tradition — Myrddin, Aneirin, and Taliesin — are all legendary characters from the Old North.

During the early tenth century, the lesser English kingdoms were merged into one greater England. A century and a half later, this substantial kingdom was ripe for the picking when the Normans invaded in 1066, imposing their own aristocracy upon the Anglo-Saxons and founding what became the Anglo-Norman state. But the Norman lords weren't just interested in conquering England; they also wanted Ireland, Scotland and Wales.

By the time Llywarch ap Llywelyn was beginning his bardic career in the 1170s, the Normans had been making forays into the Welsh kingdoms for about a century. They built fortifications from which to attack the surrounding countryside and then flee when the Welsh could muster the will to kick them out. After the relative ease with which they had conquered England, for the first two centuries at least, Wales proved to be a much more laborious task. As a court bard, Llywarch ap Llywelyn would have been witness to a strong and independent Welsh nobility, fighting off the most recent wave of invaders from the East.

As is often the case with mediaevel court bards, we know very little about Llywarch. Like Taliesin, all we can say of him is inferred from the 30 poems that have come down to us, a small part of his entire output over a long career. All the surviving poems are addressed to the nobility of the kingdom of Gwynedd in North West Wales. These were no different to noblemen in other mediaevel aristocracies, riven as they were by internecine conflict that saw brothers, cousins and uncles slaying, imprisoning or betraying each other. And the prize they fought over was not just Gwynedd itself, but the whole of Wales. The royal lineage of Gwynedd claimed supremacy over all other Welsh kingdoms, which made the kingship a most coveted prize. Having praised, threatened and commemorated several Gwynedd aristocrats in highly wrought and elegant poetry, during the 1180s, his second decade as a court bard, Llywarch came into the service of a young nobleman by the name of Llywelyn ab Iorwerth, a leader who would become the greatest Welsh king of his age.

Llywarch praised Llywelyn several times in his youth, celebrating his coming of age in a poem which depicts him as the king who will wed the land. In the middle section of the poem, Llywarch says:

> Your praise poets are beautiful in your fair retinue,
>
> Your sword has spread your fame.
>
> Your weapons — sudden death for enemies —
>
> You have mastered them, oppressor of foes.
>
> Your great merit earns you
>
> A betrothal with the nature of the kingdom
>
> And a long marriage to the Island of Britain . . .[120]

The evocation of this sovereignty myth in a public ceremony of praise once again shows how a bard could transform a mortal man into an ideal hero before the very eyes of the

---

120   My translation of the text in E.M. Jones and N.A. Jones (eds.), *Gwaith Llywarch ap Llywelyn* (UWP 1991), 174.

gathered court. The power of this depiction instills in the young nobleman a divine right to rule: he is the one and only legitimate mate that can ensure the land is defended from her enemies. The sovereignty in question, the magical bride and female body who is the symbol of the land, is Britain herself, whole and indivisible.

This speaks to the old myth of Welsh supremacy in Britain, as Llywelyn is not only the rightful groom of Gwynedd, but of the entire island to which all Welsh kings have an ancient claim. As well as Llywelyn being a perfect king, the land he is destined to marry is the perfect Britain. The poem marked a powerful moment in the young man's journey from mere mortal ruler of a fractious territory to the mythic future king of a united and sovereign isle.

The bardic power of awen was not only used to raise up a nobleman as a paragon of kingship, but also to cast him down when the need arose. Llywarch ap Llywelyn is one of the few bards to have a poetic threat recorded in manuscript. That is, a poem that was composed not in praise of a nobleman, but to warn him of publicly offending the bard. Such a poem could besmirch one's good name, and therefore not something a nobleman wished to preserve in the court archives, the likely reason so few have survived. But for whatever reason, Llywarch's warning to Gruffydd ap Cynan ab Owain,[121] Llywelyn's older

---

121   GRIFF-ith ap KUN-an ab OW-ine;'un' as in 'sun.

cousin, was preserved for later generations to see. It's not a satire, but a threat to cause shame should Gruffydd not abide by Llywarch's request:

> Heaven's Maintainer, raise up my ability,
>
> Lord God, born a Man,
>
> Hear my request for a gift
>
> Should my song issue from your blessing,
> from your message.
>
> Do not, generous Lord in possession of divinity,
>
> Leave me, nor take me from You.
>
> With my talent for words, through Your grace was I made;
>
> Its light persists about one or another:
>
> So it is for a generous and brave man of great fame,
>
> So also for a miser in his ignominy and sorrow.[122]

The idea here is to impress upon Gruffydd the fact that Llywarch has direct access to the divine power of awen, something that flows from God's blessing. Not only that, but this magical awen can surround the subject of a poem like a persistent light, regardless of whether it's praise for the worthy or a warning to a 'miser'. Llywarch encourages Gruffydd to pay attention to his words:

---

122 My translation of the text in Jones & Jones (1991), 80.

> And you, such an angry fighter of battles,
>
> Cruel [one], enjoying fair poetry —
>
> In your case, may the casting of my poem not be
>
> Like casting pearls before swine.

The last line here, which is of course in reference to Matthew 7:6, could well be the source of Llywarch's bardic pseudonym, *Prydydd y Moch*, 'Bard of the Pigs'. The bardic guilds appear to have been rife with leg pulling, and although most court bards had quite respectable pseudonyms, a few had been christened with some rather unfortunate ones. Llywarch's own pseudonym suggests that Gruffydd may not have heeded the warning, resulting in the poem truly being 'a pearl cast before swine'.

> So consider, chief lord, how expensive
>
> The gold of Arabia is, if I request it.
>
> Contemptible men do not consider my radiance
> in my poetry,
>
> Send them away from you in shame!
>
> And if you do not send them, I will cause a reddening
>
> To appear on your face, to follow you
> with great embarrassment,
>
> And your grandsons will feel it following them,

And your great grandsons; [I shall cause it]
in my adversity, in my indignation.

And here, you have a free choice,

Either shame or praise will accompany me to your court.[123]

The issue appears to be Gruffydd's patronage of lowly minstrels, perhaps to lower his entertainment costs. As a result, he would have broken the monopoly the bardic guilds had on patronage by employing those who weren't trained in the formal mysteries of awen. These common buskers appear to have offended Llywarch, perhaps scorning his official status and not paying him his due respect. If Gruffydd does not eject the riffraff and abide by the guild's rules, Llywarch will curse him and his descendants with a red face. This is one of the few recorded examples of the divine awen being used to curse, although we can assume it was a more common occurrence than such rare accounts would otherwise lead us to believe.

Llywarch ap Llywelyn used the bardic power of awen to influence the nobility of his day, so it needed to be a powerful force that could really do things in the world. His awen was directed at very powerful men, and as several scholars have noted, it was always in service of a greater cause, that of the kingdom of Gwynedd. Llywarch would have praised anyone who could unite the land, defend its interests and ensure its

---

123   Ibid.

survival in a violent, feudal age. He likewise was prepared to threaten anyone who would subvert the power of the bardic guilds. It was, after all, one of the few cultural institutions that upheld the values of the heroic ideal and ensured certain moral standards were observed by the nobility. His awen was used to pursue a political stability that would benefit his fellow country-folk and maintain the dignity and honour of his nation.

We only have one poem where Llywarch explicitly uses his awen for personal gain, and in circumstances that we can well understand. At some stage in his career, Llywarch was accused of murder. It's unknown whether he was guilty or innocent, but it appears as if there wasn't enough evidence to prove the case either way, and the matter appeared to hang on Llywarch's word alone. When such troublesome cases arose in the mediaevel period, it was common practice to evoke God as the ultimate arbiter of justice. This was done by making the accused submit to a trial where God's favour or displeasure could be divined. In Llywarch's case, the trial was a painful one. After fasting for three days, he would have been required to grasp a red-hot rod of iron in his hand, take three steps while still holding it and then put it down. His hand would then have been bound for three days, after which time it was inspected. If the wound was clean and healing, it showed God favoured him and he would have been proclaimed innocent. If infected, it was a sign God was not on his side. He would have been found guilty and suffered the full punishment under the law. One of the most intriguing of Llywarch's poems to have survived appears to be a prayer to God declaimed just before he faced this ordeal:

Heaven's Creator, true to His servant,

I trust in this as I would in John's [Gospel].

A hard judge according to the given laws God created:

I am obedient to You as my maintainer.

Your truth shines white hot;

Your ardour is not hostile to my intent.

Consider, as You judge my lineage.

Creature of burning pain, what created you?

I beseech Peter, who is in Christ's family,

He that bore the cross with dignity,

By the fair entreaty of St Thomas's intercession,

And that of Philip and Paul and Andrew,

Through the grip of my hand, blue-white blade,

To avoid responsibility for murder,

Good iron, testify: when Madog

Was murdered, it was not by my hand,

More than Cain and his followers

Can have a share in heaven and its nine kingdoms.

For my part, I wish for friendship,

God's favour upon me, and escape from His wrath.[124]

We can well imagine Llywarch ap Llywelyn, the court bard of the king of Gwynedd, chanting his bardic prayer before the ordeal to call upon God's grace. It may have been odd if one trained in the mysteries of the divine awen had not taken advantage of his direct connection to God. As opposed to using poetry to mythologise a patron or threaten a foe with a curse, this time Llywarch used it to direct his awen back to its source with a plea to prove his innocence. We can only assume that this use of bardic power was successful, as Llywarch appears to have continued in service of Llywelyn for some decades to come.

He would bear witness to Llywelyn becoming the most powerful Welsh king of his age and earn the honorific of Llywelyn the Great. After uniting Gwynedd, Llywelyn persisted in seeking greater and greater influence, gaining enough territory and support amongst the Welsh nobility to become the dominant power in Wales. In 1216 he held a council in Aberdyfi, just north of Borth where the infant Taliesin was discovered, to apportion lands to his followers amongst the

---

124 Ibid. 146-52.

lesser princes of Wales. The bard's myth-making had evidently rubbed off on the nobleman, instilling in Llywelyn enough of a thirst for greatness to pursue his ambitions.

The following year, Llywarch sang his praises for the last time. Llywelyn would consolidate his power for another twenty years, but we hear nothing more of Llywarch in relation to the great king. In the opening lines of that last poem to his king, the aged bard defines his relationship to Llywelyn in comparison to Taliesin's relationship to Elffin:

> I beseech my Lord for awen of splendid greeting,
>
> The words of Ceridwen, lady of poetry,
>
> In the mode of Taliesin releasing Elffin,
>
> In the manner of the bardic mysteries
> of the bards' adulation.[125]

As always, the poem opens with a plea to God for awen, followed by an acknowledgement of the other source of bardic power, Ceridwen, the lady of poetry who made a potion of awen from the magic herbs growing wild in God's creation. Again, we see a rather skilful negotiation between the native mythology and the official religion of the time, showing how both were not only important sources of bardic power, but that the one didn't contradict the other.

---

125   Ibid. 247-59.

In the third line, Llywarch claims that his service to Llywelyn is akin to the episode where Taliesin reveals his power at Maelgwn's court, releasing his patron, Elffin, from wrongful imprisonment. This is quite the claim, as it portrays Llywelyn as a nobleman who shouldn't disregard Llywarch's bardic power lest he become a victim of his political opponents. By implication, Llywarch is positioning himself as the saviour and defender of his patron, the king.

As with all good poetry, certain phrases evoke more than one meaning, and these are often lost in translation. The original Welsh of the last line above can be translated as:

| *Yn nyllest* | *barddrin* | *beirdd fanieri.* |
| In the manner of | the bardic mysteries | [of the] bards' cries [of adulation]. |

The last word, *banieri,* is the plural of *baniar,* which literally means 'cry' or 'shout' and figuratively 'praise'. What's implied is a crying out of bardic praise, a powerful voicing of adulation, not that dissimilar to the powerful storm of wind that's depicted in the later folktale. For Llywarch, this is the active force of awen in the king's court, praise that frees the patron from the confines of the mundane, setting him above the tangled web of courtly politics. Llywarch's claim, like that of all court bards, was that this could be achieved by force of imagination, a mythologising of the patron in public, raising him up for all to see as a perfected man, a true embodiment of the ideal king.

These were the manifest effects of the bardic mysteries, the secret knowledge of how awen could transform the world.

CHAPTER 6

The Cauldron

. . . put the cauldron on a fire, keeping it at a constant heat,

and boil it day and night for a year and a day,

after which time three drops of the essence of

the many plants would be ready.

It's no accident that Ceridwen's cauldron is a primary source of the Welsh bard's awen. The cauldron is a very ancient symbol that's found throughout the Celtic tradition, providing, as it did, a central focus in the lives of families and communities for millennia. Eating together is one of the most satisfying ways of keeping company, and the cauldron and its fire would have been a natural place to talk, gossip, tell stories, sing and perform. It not only provided physical sustenance, but it also fed the soul. Some of the most exquisite examples of ancient Celtic art can be found on cauldrons; they were ceremonial vessels used at the highest levels of Celtic society, playing a part in celebrations and rituals alike.

The mediaevel Welsh inherited this rich cultural heritage, and as a result, Ceridwen's cauldron stands for many things. As in the Irish tradition,[126] some bards saw it as a symbol for their tradition, and in this sense, it can be understood as having two parts: the container and its contents. The container, the physical body of the symbolic cauldron, comprises all the practical elements of the bardic craft, all of those things that were taught to bardic apprentices. For as long as the Cymry have been a people, Welsh bards have specialised in the composition of verse in strict and complex meters brimming with musical effects. This bardic craft of poetry, *cerdd dafod*[127] ('tongue craft'), requires a great deal of discipline, just like learning to play any classical instrument to a high standard. This craft is the body of the cauldron, it's a container that holds the contents of the Welsh bardic tradition, as described in the work of Elidir Sais,[128] an eminent bard of the early thirteenth century:

> *Llathraid fy marddair wedi Myrddin,*
>
> *Llethrid a berid o bair awen.*
>
> Bright my poetry in the manner of Myrddin,
>
> A brightness caused by the cauldron of awen.[129]

---

126   For example, in the Irish poem 'The Cauldron of Poesy', discussed in detail on the online course which you can follow at https://celticsource.online/taliesin-origins

127   Kerth DAV-od.

128   El-ID-eer Sice; 'ice' as in 'nice'.

129   My translation of the text in R. Geraint Gruffydd (ed.) *Gwaith Meilyr Brydydd a'i ddisgynyddion* (UWP 1994), 337.

The implication here is that through the study required by his tradition, Elidir Sais has learned to emulate the work of great bardic masters such as Myrddin. The bardic tradition has taught him to bring a shine to his work, to make it bright like the best poems preserved by the bards. In the second line, this same brightness is also caused by Ceridwen's cauldron. For Elidir Sais, the tradition and the cauldron of awen appear to be one and the same, both bringing the same brightness to his poetry.

Like all court poets of his time, Elidir's work was composed for its sound as much as for its meaning. If we focus on the craft of the original Welsh lines, we can find many types of ornamentation, perhaps the most obvious being alliteration, that is repeating consonants in one line:

> Llathraid fy **m**ard**d**air wedi **M**yr**dd**in,
>
> Llethrid a **b**e**r**id o **b**ai**r** awen.[130]

The alliteration of **m** and **rdd** in the last two-thirds of the first line stresses the meaning: fy **m**ard**d**air — 'my poetry' chiming in sound with a source of that very poetry, that being **M**yr**dd**in. Then, in the second line, we see how the alliteration of **b** and **r** is linked with the internal rhyming of id. This is a standard formula within a line of poetry that's still used in Welsh poetry

---

130   LLATH-ride vu MARDD-ire WED-i MERTH-in, / LLETH-rid a BER-id o bire awen.

today,[131] as are a numerous array of other arrangements of accent, alliteration and internal rhyme. There is also alliteration connecting the first words of both lines, which means almost all the consonants used are repeated elsewhere, giving the whole poetic sentence a type of audible symmetry:

> **Llathr**aid *fy marddair wedi Myrddin,*
>
> **Llethr**id *a berid o bair awen.*

This quick example should give some insight into the complexity of the bardic arts, a craft that continues to evolve to this day.[132]

The oral body of traditional poetry apprentice bards had to memorise was a substantial part of their training. These old poems were thought to have been composed by ancient bardic masters such as Myrddin, Taliesin and Aneirin, passed down the generations from teacher to apprentice. Both components of the Welsh bardic tradition — the complex poetic craft and the ancient body of oral poetry — supported each other. A knowledge of poetic technique, grammar, vocabulary and a feel for how these elements could be combined, allowed the apprentice to appreciate the works of the old masters, while those works in turn, memorised as they were and practised as pieces for public declamation, were examples of what poetry should sound

---

131   Technically known as a *cynghanedd sain*, or 'sound harmony'.

132   A full account of this craft in English has been given by Mererid Hopwood in *Singing in Chains* (Gomer 2016).

like. We find echoes of sixth-century poetry in poems of the twelfth century, which means successive generations of bardic apprentices knew the work of the ancient masters well enough for it to have been a natural quarry for them.

Once the craft of poetry had been mastered and the works of past masters memorised, the cauldron of tradition had been soundly fashioned. But what of the second part of the symbolic cauldron, its contents? In very simple terms, the tradition would have become a source of inspiration for apprentices, enabling them to compose new work from within its stable confines. Just like the oral tradition, Ceridwen's cauldron is a durable container within which is found the refined essence of awen, the divine inspiration that confers spiritual insight and the ability to conjure exquisite poetry. Gwion's diligent keeping of the cauldron produces a potent brew of magical nourishment, a very fitting metaphor for the education an apprentice bard would have undergone, bringing the heat of new life to the cold iron of the tradition, finally imbibing a potent distillation that comes out of the preceding centuries of poetic art. In this sense, it may not be an accident that some aspects of bardic lore were preserved as triads, emulating the 'three drops of inspiration' produced by the symbolic cauldron.

Yet this is but one interpretation of the ancient cauldron drawn from a few brief words in the work of one court bard. The peculiar quality of any symbol is it suggests many meanings that are all available at the same time. Even though the interpretation above makes sense within the terms of the Welsh bardic tradition, the symbol of the cauldron also belongs to an extensive mythology that runs through many other related traditions and cultures. This mythology revolves around the idea of magical food and the way it alters human consciousness. After all, the thing that confers magical enlightenment upon the bard is what the cauldron produces, the magical potion taken into the body as a spiritual sustenance.

Whereas in Elis Gruffydd's version of the folktale where Gwion Bach pushes Morfran out of the way, in John Jones' version, the three drops simply leap out of the cauldron and land on Gwion Bach's finger. These being scalding hot he puts his finger in his mouth; as instinctive a response as any. But that very simple action ties the story into a very ancient myth that permeates many stories from the Celtic lands.[133] Sometimes the finger is burned on a snake or a salmon, or as in one fifteenth-century poem, Gwion Bach put his whole hand in the boiling cauldron.[134] Acquiring magical knowledge was a painful event

---

133   See Juliette Wood, 'The Folklore Background of the Gwion Bach Section of Hanes Taliesin', *Bulletin of the Board of Celtic Studies* Vol. 39, Part 4 (May 1982), 621-34.

134   Thomas Roberts & Ifor Williams (eds.), *The Poetical Works of Dafydd Nanmor* (UWP, 1923),110.

that caused an instinctive reaction. It's that response to pain that actually gets the potent awen into Gwion Bach's mouth. This appears to be the very old idea that captivated so many Celtic storytellers and audiences.

Perhaps the most obvious narrative that can be compared to *The Tale of Taliesin* is the Irish story of Finn's poetic enlightenment.[135] The Irish manuscript that preserves it is likely from the twelfth century, but the story itself may go back to the ninth or even the eighth. Finn is one of those magical babes that are found in myths from across the world, their standout talent being able to accomplish in their swaddling clothes things most adults would find challenging. Their infant exploits are a precursor to their marvels in maturity, and Finn is no different in his ability to impress those who turn up to guide him. Soon after Finn's birth, a powerful female druid by the name of Bodhmall adopts him. One day, the boy comes across Bodhmall and her companion trying to catch a deer.

> 'Alas', said the two old women, 'we cannot manage to catch one of them yonder.' 'I can', replied the then unnamed Finn, and he rushed at them, and caught two of

---

135 A discussion on the similarities can be found in the introduction to Ford (1992), 17-30. Another comparable Irish story is that of Cearbhall O Dálaigh, see James E. Doan 'Cearbhall O Dálaigh as Archetypal Poet in Irish Folk Tradition', *Proceedings of the Harvard Celtic Colloquium*, 1981, Vol. 1 (1981), 95-123.

the stags and brought them with him. There was not, at
that time, any hunter equal to him.[136]

Apart from the period of childhood being connected to hunting and a spiritually potent woman, the more obvious similarity between Taliesin and Finn can be found in the episode concerning the poet Finneces. As is so often the case in the storytelling traditions of Europe, hunting precedes an encounter with supernature:

> *Finn went to study poetry with Finneces, who dwelt*
> *beside the Boyne. Finneces had spent seven years beside*
> *the Boyne, waiting for the salmon of Linn Fec . . . for it*
> *had been prophesied to him that he would consume the*
> *salmon of Fec, and that after that there would be nothing*
> *which he did not know. The salmon was caught and was*
> *entrusted to the boy to cook, and the poet told him not to*
> *eat any of it. The lad brought the salmon to him after he*
> *had cooked it. 'Did you eat any of the salmon, lad?' said*
> *the poet. 'No,' said the lad, 'but I burnt my thumb and put*
> *it in my mouth after that.' 'Finn is your name, lad,' he said.*
> *'And it is you who are destined to eat the salmon. Truly,*
> *you are the fair one' (in finn). The lad ate the salmon after*
> *that. That is what gave the knowledge to Finn: whenever*
> *he put his thumb in his mouth and chanted through*
> *teinm laíde [a technique of divination involving chewing*
> *flesh], what he did not know would be revealed to him.*
> *He learned the three things which qualify a poet: teinm*

---

136   John Carey (trans.), 'The Boyhood Deeds of Finn' in *The Celtic Heroic Age* edited by
John T. Koch (CSP 2013), 197.

*laíde, and imbas forosnai ['the light of illumination'], and
díchetal di channaib ['incantation over heads'].*[137]

Both the naming of the wonder child and the poetic ability he
receives by burning a finger (or thumb) on magical food are
clearly the same elements we find in the Taliesin story. In Finn's
case, the storyteller goes into a bit more detail about the special
abilities he receives, which are in fact the legal qualifications
required of a master *fili,* a professional poet of high rank.[138]

According to *Cormac's Glossary,* a ninth-century
dictionary that discusses the meaning and etymology of certain
terms, *imbas forosnai* was a divinatory practice that involved
the chewing of raw meat and communing with supernatural
powers. Although banned by St Patrick for being far too pagan,
it apparently continued for centuries after the saints decree.
The practice involved a type of trance induced by the ritual
chewing and resulted in the diviner receiving special or hidden
knowledge. The ritual is suggested in other stories about Finn,
as is the trance and the involvement of the otherworld.[139]
Because of the several variations in Finn's magic finger story,
it's likely to be of great age in Irish culture. For there to be
variations, there needs to be time for them to evolve.

---

137   Carey (2013), 198.

138   John Carey, 'The Three Things Required of a Poet', *Ériu* Vol. 48 (1997), 41-58.

139   See Nora K. Chadwick, 'Imbas Forosnai', *Scottish Gaelic Studies* Vol. 4, part 2 (OUP 1935), 97-135.

It's impossible to say for certain why the stories of Taliesin and Finn are similar, but there are at least two possibilities: either one culture borrowed from the other or both inherited the same basic idea from a common ancestor. According to a new theory,[140] the Indo-European ancestors of the Celts reached the western seaboard of Europe around four and a half thousand years ago. Soon after, their language developed into an early form of Celtic. Around three thousand years ago, this early Celtic split into two branches, one becoming Irish and the other Welsh. This means that both cultures share a common inheritance in the earlier Indo-European culture, so similarities in their myths, such as those we find in the stories of Taliesin and Finn, may reveal that common inheritance. The Celtic concept of a wonder child receiving poetic enlightenment by consuming magical food is potentially three thousand years old.

We can also look at other related traditions for stories about magical foods that confer a poetic ability. Norse is a cousin of the Celtic languages on the Indo-European family tree, and in one of its classic texts, the *Younger Edda*, written in the thirteenth century, we find the story of Odin stealing the Mead of Poetry. In Norse myth, the Aesir and the Vanir are warring tribes of gods, and in the story they come together to seek peace:

---

140   For a summary, see Barry Cunliffe's chapter 'The Arrival of the Indo-European Languages' in his book *The Ancient Celts* (OUP 2018).

> *... and they appointed a peace-conference and made a*
> *truce by this procedure, that both sides went up to a vat*
> *and spat their spittle into it. But when they dispersed, the*
> *gods kept this symbol of truce and decided not to let it be*
> *wasted, and out of it made a man. His name was Kvasir.*
> *He was so wise that no one could ask him any questions*
> *to which he did not know the answer.*[141]

This is the origin story of the first poet, or the first *skald* as it would have been in the Norse of the time. It's no accident that the first poet, a being who embodies all knowledge, was created at a time of peace when the warrior class had put down their arms, giving opportunity for culture to flourish. When we consider Taliesin's legend, he is likewise a being of complete knowledge, even 'the teacher of the whole universe' as he claims in the folktale. Like Kvasir, he is also involved in competitions of knowledge, challenging people with hard questions that only he knows how to answer. But this is just the beginning of our story, because Kvasir was

> *... treacherously murdered by the dwarves, Fjalar and*
> *Galar, who by mixing up his blood with honey, composed*
> *a liquor of such surpassing excellence that whoever*
> *drinks of it acquires the gift of song.*[142]

---

141 Anothony Faulkes (trans.), *Snorri Sturluson: Edda* (Everyman 2008), 61-2.

142 Ibid. 62.

This echoes the imagery we find in *The Book of Taliesin*, where the great bard claims to have been brewed and then set before a king:

> I was matured,
>
> I was a drink served to a ruler,
>
> I was dead, I was alive,
>
> Stirred by a stick;
>
> I was on the sediment,
>
> Separated out from it, I was whole;[143]
>
> And the goblet gave heart, . . .[144]

The linguist Eric Hamp theorised that the name Gwion may derive from an earlier Indo-European word, *wiso*, meaning poison.[145] We may be able to catch a glimpse of an earlier myth here. That Taliesin, Gwion and Kvasir all show signs of being symbolic substances to be consumed, suggests they can all be understood as a type of spirit that, when imbibed, took possession of the imbiber.

As we shall explore further in a later chapter, the mythical bard becomes the voice of the tradition itself,

---

143   This section appears to describe the process of brewing.

144   My translation of the text in Haycock (2015), 122-3.

145   Eric P. Hamp, 'Varia II', *Eriu* Vol. 29 (1978), 152-3.

instilling inspiration wherever he is invited. In both Welsh and Norse traditions, the divinely inspired words declaimed in celebration of the heroic ideal were perhaps thought of as a type of intoxication in their own right. As we shall see, becoming the very substance that confers inspiration is very much in keeping with the Welsh bardic mythology.

In the *Younger Edda*, the magical brew that's created out of Kvasir's blood is taken by Suttung — a giant in Norse myth — and kept by his sister, the supernatural woman Gunnlod. It comes to the attention of Odin, who rather fancies a draught of the magic brew of complete knowledge, so he breaks into the cave where the mead is kept by drilling a hole into the mountain and transforming himself into a snake to crawl through. There he seduces Gunnlod:

> *[Odin] went to where Gunnlod was and lay with her for three nights and then she let him drink three draughts of the mead. In the first draught he drank everything out of [the first vat] Odrerir, and in the second out of Bodn, in the third out of Son, and then he had all the mead. Then he turned himself into the form of an eagle and flew as hard as he could. And when Suttung saw the eagle's flight he got his own eagle shape and flew after him. And when the Aesir saw Odin flying they put their containers out in the courtyard, and when Odin came in over Asgard he spat out the mead into the containers, but it was such a close thing for him that Suttung might have caught him that he sent some of the mead out backwards, and this was*

*disregarded. Anyone took it that wanted it, and it is what
we call the rhymester's share. But Odin gave Suttung's
mead to the Aesir and to those people who are skilled at
composing poetry. Thus we call poetry Odin's booty and
find, and his drink and his gift and the Aesir's drink.*[146]

With a good dose of toilet humour, this is clearly a story
to entertain an audience in their cups. There is an obvious
similarity with *The Tale of Taliesin*, particularly the hunt scene
following the taking of the special substance, where both hunter
and hunted are transformed into animals. Magical inspiration
appears to confer the ability to change shape, but the poet
also suffers the fate of almost all wild animals in becoming
prey. As with Gwion Bach being hunted by Ceridwen, Taliesin
acknowledging all of his past lives and Kvasir being murdered
for his potent blood, one of the profoundest themes to recur in
these tales is that of mortality.

In *The Tale of Taliesin,* at least, the stark acknowledgement
that all life turns to death appears to be a fundamental part
of the vision given by the magic brew. The magical substance's
transformative power is, perhaps, the same power that turns
the cycle of life and death. In Gwion Bach's desperate flight,
the potion of awen only speeds his journey to his own death,
spinning the wheel of transformation ever faster, resulting
in his unavoidable yet necessary end. Without that death,

---

146   Ibid. 62-3.

Gwion cannot become Taliesin, and neither can Kvasir's gift of knowledge be shared. The full power of the magic brew can not be realised without passing through the ultimate transformation of death.

Elsewhere in the Norse tradition, some Celtic scholars have noted the similarity between the stories of Finn and the hero Sigurd,[147] also called Siegfried in broader Germanic culture. There is one significant similarity that bears on our understanding of Taliesin's tale, that being an episode from the Völsunga Saga, another thirteenth-century text written in Old Norse. Sigurd has been fighting a dragon called Fafnir:

> Therewith, Sigurd cut out the heart of the worm with a sword called Ridil. But Regin drank of Fafnir's blood and spake, 'Grant me a boon, Sigurd, and do a thing little for thee to do. Bear the heart to the fire and roast it and give me thereof to eat.' Then Sigurd went his way and roasted it on a rod and when the blood bubbled out, he laid his finger thereon to assay it, and to check it to see if it were fully done, and then he set his finger in his mouth and lo, when the heart blood of the worm touched his tongue, straight away he knew the voice of all fowls, and all the birds, and heard with all how the woodpeckers chattered in the break beside him.[148]

---

147   See J.F. Nagy 'Intervention and Disruption in the Myths of Finn and Sigurd', *Ériu* Vol. 31 (1980), 123-131.

148   William Morris & Eirikr Magnusson (trans.), *From the Volsunga Saga* (1870), Chapter XIX.

It's not just that Sigurd can understand the language of the birds, but they relate wisdom to him and he grows wise. The flesh of this mythic beast is the manifestation of the supernatural in the natural realm, and just as natural food makes the natural body strong, so the same logic applies to supernatural food that nourishes the soul. It's a little more explicit in Sigurd's case as a dragon is a purely mythical beast, an animal that only exists in the realm of imagination and inspiration. It would naturally follow that such a beast had an effect on those faculties if we were to consume its heart.

This points to a peculiar quality of all of these symbols: the potion, salmon and the dragon's heart. As symbols, they all stand for the attaining of a greater awareness and a greater realm of meaning. That is, they are describing the very function of symbols themselves. A symbol contains within itself the potential to change our awareness, to realise that beyond its surface meaning it contains a depth of other potential meanings. The potion of awen isn't just some weird substance that makes Gwion Bach a clever poet, it changes his awareness and awakens in him the creative force of awen. In the same way, a symbol changes our awareness of what it is as it awakens our imagination.

These stories have the potential to be a spiritual food. As we consume them, we can be inspired by encountering their depth of meaning. As we ponder them, our imaginations can be nourished by their deeper perspectives. We can not only draw out the philosophical meaning in an abstracted, intellectual sense, but are also invited to immerse ourselves in the story and the complex of human experiences that give it shape. In this way, myths are not simply riddles to be solved, but the life of their characters also permeates them, giving them at least the potential to live in our imaginations. It's this ability of the imagination to breathe new life into the cold words of the page that can give myths an ageless quality. As they are resurrected time and again in our imaginations, they appear to be able resist the natural entropy of time. So long as there is an imagination to receive them, they will continue to be meaningful for countless generations. They may not be technically eternal, but they are certainly long lived.

The magical substances we have looked at are proof of this, as the very idea of them is very old in the Indo-European tradition. One of the great classics of Indian culture is the *Rig Veda*, probably first written down 2500 years ago. There are ten mandalas (sections) of the *Rig Veda* and all contain hymns to many different deities as well as to a spiritual substance known as Soma. The ninth mandala is dedicated exclusively to Soma, suggesting its pre-eminence for the Vedic poets. For example, in Hymn 48, we read:

> We have drunk Soma and become immortal;

We have attained the light the Gods discovered.

Now, what may the enemy's malice do to harm us?

What, O Immortal, mortal man's deception?

May we enjoy with an enlivened spirit

The juice thou givest, like ancestral riches.

O Soma, King, prolong thou our existence . . . [149]

Soma here is a magical drink that gives access to *ancestral riches*, a substance that enables a transcendence of time. In this sense, it's like another magical substance in the Vedic tradition, that being amrita. In the related Buddhist tradition, we also find allusions to a special nectar that bears some resemblance to both magical drinks. Beyond the Indo-European tradition, the Taoists of China were eternally cooking up different stews of immortality and the alchemists in Europe attempted various concoctions intended to have similar results.

What appears to be common to many of these substances is the idea of immortality, the ability to transcend time, to step out of the temporal realm. Taliesin comes into the world in full possession of the magical enlightenment he gained in his past life as Gwion Bach. If we also include the countless transformations described in the legendary poems, then he also possesses all the wisdom gleaned during all of his past

---

149 Ralph T.H. Griffith (trans.), *Rig Veda* (1896), Hymn XLVIII.

incarnations, as suggested in the opening section of 'The Battle of the Trees':

> I was in many forms
>
> Before I was unfettered.
>
> I was a slender, mottled sword
>
> Made by hand.
>
> I was a tear-drop in the air,
>
> I was the light of the stars.
>
> I was a written word,
>
> I was a book in my prime.
>
> I was a lantern's light
>
> For a year and a half.
>
> I was a bridge traversed
>
> Over sixty estuaries.
>
> I was a path; I was an eagle,
>
> I was a coracle on the seas.
>
> I was a bubbling in drink,
>
> I was a raindrop in a shower.[150]

---

150   My translation of the text in Haycock (2015), 174.

One of Taliesin's claims is that his memory reaches all the way back to the beginning of time. His vision is that of his own immortal soul present in all things, his wisdom encompassing all of creation.

At the heart of all these myths is the rather obvious fact that humans have always enjoyed altering their consciousness by ingesting certain substances. The mead of poetry in Norse myth has an obvious counterpart in the Welsh tradition, not only as a ceremonial drink, but as a drink that could literally loosen one's tongue. Perhaps one of the easiest interpretations we can make of Ceridwen's cauldron is that it really is a witch's cauldron for the brewing of actual potions. The Ceridwen of the folktale has many things in common with the stereotypical witch found elsewhere in the same period.

In Shakespeare's *Macbeth*, we find three weird sisters chanting their spells over a bubbling cauldron full of rather disgusting ingredients. But there was indeed some historical truth to this stereotype of the potion-brewing witch. Allowing for the diversity of witchcraft across Europe, we find some common traits that appear to explain parts of Taliesin's folktale quite well. Before turning to the sources, it's important to remember that these accounts are often given from the rather paranoid position of a reactionary Christianity.

The drawn image was one of the more powerful ways mediaevel authors presented their rather cartoonish vision of the witch. In his 1489 thesis *Of Witches and Diviner Women*, the Austrian Ulrich Molitor includes drawings of witches working over cauldrons, brewing up potions, ointments and salves: what were in reality the bread and butter of folk healers and wise women. The other significant feature in these images is that, after taking the potion, the witches appear to transform into animals.

The witches of western Europe knew how to brew hallucinogenic potions. The sources that describe these potions range over a period of centuries, and refer sometimes to an oil the witches used to transport themselves to their gatherings, known as The Witches' Sabbat. The subject came to the attention of modern readers in the work of Michael Harner, who researched the role of hallucinogenic plants in European witchcraft.[151] Harner collated a fair amount of earlier research, a significant portion of which had been carried out by the anthropologist and folklorist Margaret Murray. She presented some very interesting sources, such as the following, which describes a 'greenish oil' used by witches of the seventeenth century. This is first-hand testimony given by a witness called Elizabeth Style:

> 'Before they are carried to their meetings, they anoint
> their Foreheads and Hanckwrists with an Oyl the
> Spirit brings them (which smells raw) and then they are
> carried in a very short time, using these words as they
> pass, Thout, tout a tout, tout, throughout and about. And
> when they go off from their Meetings, they say, Renfum,
> Tormentum . . . , . . . all are carried to their several homes
> in a short space.'[152]

Although containing a lot of valuable material, by today some of Harner's conclusions have been found wanting, even though

---

151   See 'The Role of Hallucinogenic Plants in European Witchcraft' in Michael Harner (ed.), *Hallucinogens and Shamanism* (1973), 131.

152   See Margaret Murray, *The Witch-Cult in Western Europe* (OUP 1962), 101-2.

his fundamental theory that witches brewed hallucinogenic substances holds true.[153] What's so intriguing about these substances is the specific effects they had, causing those who used them to imagine themselves transforming into animals such as wolves, birds or reptiles. In a university thesis on Welsh witchcraft, Sally Parkin states:

> *Hallucinogens are specific in their effect as they induce a reaction in any individual which is always the same. The predominance of chemicals such as scopolamine, hyoscyamine and atropine, substances found in the chemical composition of the narcotic elements in the [witches'] ointments, indicates specificity. Atropine induces experiences of lycanthropy (shape changing into a wolf, the probable origin of the werewolf myth) and shape transformation, whereas scopolamine induces the highly specific hallucination of growing fur, feathers, scales or warts, of feeling that one has become a particular animal, and hyoscyamine produces the specific hallucination of flight.[154]*

These hallucinogenic ointments were the products of a sophisticated herbalism. Even though many contained potent poisons, they also included different blood thinners so that the witches wouldn't become sick from too much use. These

---

153   See Tom Hatsis, 'Those Goddamn ointments: Four histories', *Journal of Psychedelic Studies* 3 (2019), 164–178.

154   S. Parkin, *Defining the Figure of the Welsh Witch, 1536-1736* (Thesis, 2002), 71; See also F.G. Surawicz, 'Lycanthropy revisited', *The Canadian Psychiatric Association Journal* Nov. 1975 (7), 537-42.

were skilled herbalists who were inducing particular types of hallucination in as safe and controlled a manner as they could achieve given their resources.

Considering this, there are a few important questions that we should ask. Alongside similarities to other myths, was Ceridwen's cauldron of awen at least partly based on the practice of brewing up hallucinogenic potions? Is this how Taliesin is granted his mystical visions and ability to transform? What modern studies on witchcraft have revealed is that this was indeed a culture of mystical vision, and if one thing is certain, from the legendary poems of *The Book of Taliesin* through to the sixteenth-century folktale, one of the main characteristics of the great bard is his visionary experiences as different objects and animals. From the perspective of modern anthropology, it's relatively straightforward to consider these visions as the expression of a shamanic culture that can be found across the world.

In her book *Cunning Folk and Familiar Spirits*, Emma Wilby describes British witchcraft as a visionary tradition where more frequently women, but sometimes men, sought mystical visions in which to converse with familiar spirits, demons and fairies. She concludes that this is an ancient aspect of British folk culture:

> . . . *magical belief and practice, as preserved through oral traditions, had been providing ordinary people with*

[spiritual] freedom and personal responsibility for many
thousands of years prior to the arrival of the orthodox
faith.[155]

We can assume that at least some witches in mediaeval and early modern Wales were involved in this type of mysticism. The similarity between the effects of the witch's ointment and what we find in *The Tale of Taliesin* suggests that, at least in the popular imagination, the visionary tradition of the witches was compatible with that of the Welsh bards. Even though there's no explicit reference to the use of anything much stronger than mead in the Welsh bardic tradition, the central role of a potion-brewing witch in their most important myth has some implications. Bearing in mind the antiquity of visioning practices inherited by mediaevel witchcraft, there may have been some long-standing relationship between the bardic tradition and that of the witches. This could at least be understood as one broad culture of mysticism explored by two different groups within the same society.

One question that arises from all of this is whether we can read a historical reality in Taliesin's tale? Does the story reflect real behaviours in the past? We've already seen that witches had a sophisticated knowledge of hallucinogenic substances, and the bards claimed their awen came from Ceridwen's magic

---

155   Emma Wilby, *Cunning Folk and Familiar Spirits: Shamanistic Visionary Traditions in Early Modern British Witchcraft and Magic* (SAP 2013), 256.

cauldron. Not only that, but some of the mystic visions related by Taliesin have a hallucinogenic quality. We need look no further than this sequence in 'The Battle of the Trees':

> I wounded a great, scaly beast.
>
> Upon him was a hundred heads
>
> And a stubborn host
>
> Beneath his tongue's root,
>
> And another host
>
> In [the folds of] his neck napes;
>
> A forked, black toad
>
> With a hundred claws upon him;
>
> A crested, speckled snake
>
> With a hundred sinful souls
>
> Tortured in its flesh.[156]

Were apprentice bards being sent off to steal these magic potions? Or were the bards simply regular customers to these practising herbalists? Does animal transformation and symbolic death correspond to an actual ritual? For all of the misogyny of mediaevel society, did the patriarchal bardic guilds have a symbiotic relationship with the witches of their day? Were

---

156　My translation of the text in Haycock (2015), 175-6.

female initiators having to mother male initiates back to reality, talking them down from their powerful trips? Unfortunately, until more evidence comes to light, we shall never really know.

CHAPTER 7

Transformations

. . . he transformed himself into one grain. What did Ceridwen do but transform into a short-tailed, black hen and swallowed Gwion into her womb, . . .

O ne of the most ancient themes in Celtic myth is that of animal transformation. As far back as the Celtic Iron Age, we find imagery that blends both the human and animal forms. Perhaps one of the most iconic pieces of Celtic art is the image of the horned figure on Plate A of the Gundestrup Cauldron, made about two thousand years ago.

Some assume this figure to be more of a priest than a god, the partial animal transformation suggesting a mortal man in communion with animal spirits. Others have identified the figure as Cernunnos, 'Horned One', a male deity found elsewhere in the Celtic iconography of the period. He is one amongst several horned figures, both male and female, that were used in the religious art of Celtic tribes across Europe.

The Gundestrup Cauldron image suggests a great deal about the relationship between the human and the animal, not just because the seated figure has antlers on his head, but because he is surrounded by animals and sat next to an antlered stag. If we count the tines on the antlers, we find that the seated figure has six tines, whereas the stag has seven. Common lore tells us that a stag grows one tine for every year of its life, making the stag seven years old and the seated figure six. If this is intentional, then the stag can be considered the elder of the two. The animals depicted either side of the figure — the stag and the dog both — appear to be speaking to him, perhaps whispering in his ear the combined wisdom of the hunter and the hunted. If this is the case, then a transformed human being who partakes of the wisdom of the mythical hunt was an ancient idea long before it appeared in the Taliesin myth.

Elsewhere in Celtic art, the blending of human and animal is taken a step further, such as in this piece from the temple of Nodens at Lydney Park, a Romano-Celtic site in the south-east of Wales.

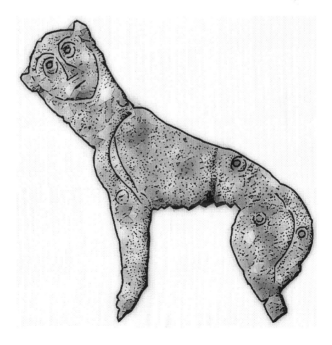

It could be as early as the first century of the common era, or perhaps as late as the fourth or fifth. The image is often interpreted as a human face on a dog's body, the dog often associated with healing gods such as Nodens. The figure can easily be part of the Brythonic tradition, that of the very early Welsh, and therefore a precursor to the many animal transformations we find in *The Book of Taliesin*.

One such transformation can be found in the poem 'Buarth Beirdd', 'The Bards' Enclosure', which could be from the late twelfth century. In the opening section, Taliesin says:

> . . . I am a druid, I am learned, I am a wordsmith,
>
> I am a serpent, I am desire, I consume.[157]

For Taliesin, his serpent nature is just as prominent as his magical and poetic qualities, his voracious appetite proof of his passion as a poet. Taliesin here is a visceral being that partakes of the animal body's nature; he's not some abstracted, pure essence that only exists in a distant otherworld. The same type of lusty physicality is expressed in another of the legendary poems from his *Book*, this time in the last section of 'Angar Kyfundawt', ('The Hostile Confederacy'):

---

157 My translation of the text in Haycock (2015), 79.

> I was a speckled white cockerel
>
> On the hens in Eidyn;
>
> I was a stallion in stud,
>
> I was a hot bull.[158]

These animals stand for fertility, desire and sexual promiscuity, and here Taliesin's animal passions infuse his bardic power. The following section tells us how he is not only the source of fecundity, but also its fruit:

> I was a grain [. . .]
>
> It grew on the hill;
>
> I'm reaped, I'm planted,
>
> I'm thrown in a kiln,
>
> I'm dropped from hand
>
> To be roasted.
>
> A hen received me,
>
> A red-clawed one, a crested foe;
>
> I rested nine nights
>
> A child in her womb.[159]

---

158   Ibid. 122.

159   Ibid. 122-3.

His experience of desire and sexual power naturally results
in his partaking of the life-cycle of all living things, and just
as he is potent in life-force, so he is also fated to die and be
reborn. Later in the Taliesin tradition, we find other animal
transformations expressing other qualities, such as this section
in a fourteenth-century poem, which describes a variation on
the animal chase scene:

> He escaped as a young roebuck
>
> Taking cover in a wood.
>
> He escaped as a wolf-cub
>
> [With a] wolf-pack in the wild.
>
> He escaped as a thrush
>
> [Speaking] the same language as the Coelwys.
>
> He escaped as a fox,
>
> Regular leap and [graceful] posture;
>
> He escaped as a pine marten
>
> — To no avail.
>
> He escaped as a squirrel,
>
> The growth [of trees] did not hide him; . . .[160]

---

160   My translation of the text in Guffydd Fôn Gruffydd (ed.), *Cerddi Taliesin Ben Beirdd y
Gorllewin I* (PhD Thesis 1997), 107.

'He escaped as a thrush / [*speaking*] *the same language as the Coelwys'* is an intriguing couplet that alludes to Taliesin speaking the Welsh dialect of the Coelwys, the people of Coel, the great-great-grandfather of Urien of Rheged. Here Taliesin (or his earlier incarnation as Gwion Bach) has transformed into a thrush, his melodious, bardic voice declaiming poetry in the old Welsh of the historical Taliesin. As we've already seen in Chapter 3, Taliesin was sometimes imagined by later poets as reincarnating as a bird, and what better form than one of the more musical song-birds. Taliesin once again partakes of the nature of the wild animals he transforms into.

Although meaning different things in different periods and in different contexts, threaded through these animal transformations is the theme of the human animal itself, an acknowledgement that the human body is but one amongst a multitude of bodies born of nature. Perhaps there is some unity throughout all the diversity, a unity that's personified in Taliesin himself. He is the eternal essence, the constant awareness that endures throughout these mutable forms.

This one witness that's present in diverse perspectives is a constant theme in Taliesin's transformations, and it suggests a few novel ideas. 'Angar Kyfundawt' ('The Hostile Confederacy') is one of the longest poems in *The Book of Taliesin*, and like several other such poems it could have been a traditional piece reworked by Llywarch ap Llywelyn, court bard to Llywelyn the Great, perhaps for performance at court as a type of high entertainment. It's typical of the legendary poems, containing transformation sequences where the mystical Taliesin relates all the different things he's been during his past lives:

> A second time I was transformed:
>
> I was a blue salmon,
>
> I was a dog, I was a stag,
>
> I was a roebuck on the mountain,
>
> I was a block, I was a spade,
>
> I was an axe in hand,
>
> I was an auger in tongs,
>
> For a year and a half.[161]

Whoever composed these lines was fascinated by the power of language to transform appearances in the mind's eye. Like the anthropomorphic visions of earlier Celtic art, in *The Book of Taliesin* the human form is shape-shifted by the powerful magic of the imagination. These poems often play with the idea that one thing can appear as another.

Of course, there is one transformation that had already taken place before these words were even uttered, and that

---

161   My translation of the text in Haycock (2015), 121-2.

was the transformation of the performing bard into the guise of the legendary Taliesin. This may have been a significant transformation in the imaginations of the audience. If it was Llywarch himself who was performing, here we have one of the highest ranking court bards of his age, bard to none other than the greatest Welsh king of his age, adopting the dramatic persona of one of the founding fathers of the bardic tradition. The bard here is mythologising himself, conflating his public persona as a court official with that of a legendary mystic, a druid-like figure from the ancient past. The effect would have been to amplify the bard's own mystique and enhance his image as the living embodiment of an ancestral lineage of wisdom-keepers. This type of cultural power would have been a priceless commodity for any bard who could channel it.

Beyond the court, the very first transformation in the myth is Gwion Bach's own magical enlightenment. The tale shows how even the most average of boys can be transformed into an enlightened sage, just as a mundane poet could be transformed into a mystic druid. Of course, Gwion's transformations don't end with the enlightenment he gained from the cauldron, any more than the performing bard's transformation ends with becoming Taliesin. Just as the bard describes his transformations into many things, in the folktale, Gwion's new powers give him the ability to change into three different animals in his attempt to escape Ceridwen. While being chased by Ceridwen, he lives life at its most intense, pursued mercilessly to the limits of physical exertion, forced to change, to adapt and transform to survive. It's unlikely that evolution as we understand it was ever a consideration in the storytelling tradition of mediaevel Wales, but a basic understanding of the instinctive drive to fight or flight is one of the simplest observations anyone could make of animal behaviour. Through his transformations, Gwion was given the opportunity to glimpse himself as one part of a living whole. All of life shares a common destiny, a common struggle for survival, and ultimately faces the final transformation of death. In experiencing the life of hunted animals Gwion was granted a hard wisdom, knowledge tempered by compassion, empathy gained through experience.

There are several other examples in the Welsh tradition of a mythic hero connected to special animals, such as the three symbolic animals in the story of St David. Born around the turn of the 500s, as a historical figure, St David, or Dewi Sant[162] as we call him in Wales, was born only one or two generations before Taliesin. But even though they don't appear

---

162   DEW-i Sant; 'e' as in 'let'.

to be connected historically, there are some striking similarities between the two legendary figures they develop into.

It may be surprising to describe Dewi Sant as a figure of Welsh myth, but the story of his life is as fantastical as anything we find in *The Tale of Taliesin*. His saint's *Life*[163] makes it quite clear that he was one of those magical infants occasionally born to the Welsh imagination. Dewi's father was a man called Sandde Bryd Angel[164] (Sandde 'Angel-face'), a king of Ceredigion in the mid-west of Wales sometime towards the end of the fifth century.

The story goes that while out hunting one day, Sandde is told by an angel to collect three different animals: a stag, a salmon, and a swarm of bees. Having got all three, he meets a nun by the name of Non and (as is sadly the case in some of these old Christian stories) rapes her, making her pregnant with the future saint. There is another Welsh infant whose birth is associated not only with a triad of wild animals but also with an unwilling mother. *The Tale of Taliesin* begins with Gwion Bach and his magical transformations into hare, salmon and bird, a triad comparable to that which precedes Dewi Sant's conception, both containing an animal from each of the domains of the Earth: land, sea and sky.

---

163   W.J. Rees, *Lives of the Cambro British Saints* (Llandovery 1853).

164   SAN-the Breed ANG-el; 'ang' as in 'hang'.

In other mediaevel texts, Dewi's father, Sandde, is twinned with a character called Morfran, as in the following list of heroes from one of *The Mabinogion* classics, *How Culhwch Won Olwen*:

> ...and Morfran son of Tegid, no man put his weapon in him... because of his ugliness, everyone assumed he was a devil helping; he had fur on him like stag's fur. And Sandde Angel Face, no man put his spear in him... because of his fairness, everyone assumed he was an angel helping.[165]

This Morfran is, of course, Morfran son of Ceridwen, as mentioned in Elis Gruffydd's version of the tale. Just as Sandde is described as Morfran's twin in *How Culhwch Won Olwen*, Gwion Bach is Morfran's twin in *The Tale of Taliesin*, taking the ugly boy's place at the cauldron and receiving the magical drops of inspiration that were intended for him. It may not be so obvious, but Gwion can also be considered Taliesin's father, becoming a seed and taken into Ceridwen's body, causing her to become pregnant. This means that both Dewi Sant and Taliesin have, in some respects at least, fathers who are both twinned with Morfran son of Ceridwen, a horribly ugly character in both texts.

---

165 My translation of the text in Rachel Bromwich & D. Simon Evans (eds.), *Culhwch ac Olwen* (UWP 1997), 8-9.

Several scholars have commented on the similarity between the figure of Morfran and two Irish characters, one by the name of Amairgen[166] and the second simply known as 'The Spirit of Poetry'.[167] In this particular story, Amairgen is a hideous boy who terrifies a poet's servant because of his demonic appearance. During the encounter Amairgen reveals his poetic skill to the servant who reports back to his master. Amairgen's father predicts that the poet will now come and kill his ugly son lest he challenge his status in a poetic contest, so he sends his son away and creates a clay effigy of him in his place.

That night, believing all to be asleep, the poet enters Amairgen's home and tries to kill him, but only breaks the clay effigy. The men of the kingdom pursue him to avenge the attack, and as recompense the poet agrees to foster Amairgen and trains him in the art of poetry. At the poet's death, Amairgen takes up his position as the pre-eminent poet of the region.[168] In the second story, the chief bard of Ireland, Senchán,[169] is just heading out on a boat trip to the Isle of Man with a party of poets, when a hideously ugly youth starts shouting at them

---

166   AV-ir-gen.

167   See Patrick K. Ford, 'The Blind, The Dumb and the Ugly', *Cambridge Mediaevel Celtic Studies* 19 (1990), 27-40; also his introduction to *Ystoria Taliesin* (1992), 21-26.

168   A full translation is given by John Carey in *The Celtic Heroic Age* edited by John T. Koch (CSP 2013), 65-6.

169   SHEN-u-kawn; 'aw' as in 'law'.

from the shore, urging Senchán to take him along and claiming the chief bard would be better off taking him than the 'vain, cocky crowd' of poets. On arriving in Man they come across a noble-looking but ragged old woman who was a great poet herself but had become stranded on the island. She challenges Senchán to complete a verse she had begun, but the stunned bard and his poets are silent. Instead, the ugly youth answers the old woman's challenge. She is then washed and dressed and taken into their party and rescued. On returning to Ireland the hideous youth has been transformed into a 'wide-eyed, mighty, royal, valorous youth', finely dressed and crowned in gold. He circles Senchán and then disappears, the story ending with the claim that he was in fact 'The Spirit of Poetry'.[170]

Both of these old Irish tales not only connect a hideous youth with poetic genius, but also suggest he symbolises a type of initiation into bardic mastery. In the story of Amairgen, a clay effigy of the youth is broken, a symbolic representation of his old self being destroyed by his bardic teacher, after which the youth is taken as his apprentice. In the story of Senchán, the transformation in the 'Spirit of Poetry' occurs only after he has been tested by the old woman, a renowned poet in her own right. In both stories the ugly boy achieves some refinement after overcoming some adversity. Likewise, Gwion achieves his refinement after the arduous encounter with Ceridwen. But in

---

170   A detailed summary can be found in Ford (1992), 22-4.

the Welsh story, the ugly youth is separated out as a twin. It appears as if the transformation of the crude into the refined is a theme of the basic myth, but whereas in the Irish stories it is the ugly youth himself who is changed, in Morfran's case, he loses out to Gwion Bach who takes on a far more promethean role. It's as if in the symbolic sequence outlined in the Welsh folktale, the initiate interrupts an otherwise closed process. There are other mentions of Morfran in the legendary poems where the ugly youth does appear to have received the potion of awen, but in the sixteenth-century folktale, he is denied the magical enlightenment.

If there's a connection between Gwion and Sandde as the fathers (strange as it may be), what of the mothers? Here again we find similarities between Non, Dewi's mother, and Ceridwen, Taliesin's mother. At first glance, they are both spiritually potent women, Non being a nun who becomes a saint in her own right, while Ceridwen is a great enchantress and the Lady of bardic inspiration (we'll explore her qualities as a goddess later on). Both women also give birth to their magic infants close to water: St Non's church, reputed to be the birthplace of Dewi Sant, sits high atop a cliff looking out to sea. Ceridwen gave her own child to a river. Both of their children continue to have a strong connection to water: Taliesin is born from the sea and in mediaeval tradition Dewi Sant is known as *Y Dyfrwr*, 'The Waterman', because of immersing himself in water as part of his ascetic practice. Dewi also caused a spring to burst forth from the ground at the moment he was baptised.

We can summarise the basic similarities between both tales like this:

1. A male who is twinned with the ugly Morfran

2. receives divine knowledge,

3. after which appear three animals: one of land, one of water, one of air.

4. This male then gets a spiritually powerful woman pregnant;

5. the resulting child's birth is connected with water,

6. and he grows to become the pre-eminent spiritual leader of his people.

So why are these tales similar? Why are two of the most important figures in Welsh cultural history conceived and born in similar circumstances? Some elements outlined above (the Morfran-twinned fathers and the three animals, for example) don't appear to be very Christian motifs, but fit rather better with the myths of folk culture. Other elements appear more Christian (angelic messengers, divine knowledge and holy water) although not exclusively so. Perhaps the early Christian church either absorbed some of the pagan culture of early Wales, or both Christian and pagan cultures inherited the same motifs and symbols. These may have been further consolidated as the respective traditions cross-pollinated and influenced each other. It wouldn't be unreasonable to assume that during the first millennium the story of how a special soul came into the world was common throughout Welsh culture, Christian or otherwise. It seems fitting that the birth of Dewi Sant, chief of all British saints (as he was regarded in mediaevel Wales) is described in similar mythic terms to that of Taliesin, Chief Bard of the West.

This similarity between both of Wales' great spiritual leaders also suggests their stories are older than the versions we have of them. The *Life of St David* was written in the eleventh century, and parts of the folklore it contains could well have been widespread at this time. We know that a version of *The Tale of Taliesin* existed in the twelfth century because we have poems from that period that mention it. Neither *The Tale of Taliesin* nor the *Life of Saint David* are necessarily older than the eleventh century, but they both contain elements that could be much older. One sign of this is the presence of similar things in other parts of Welsh mythology.

There are many other stories that we could draw a comparison with, but the story of Mabon son of Modron[171] in *How Culhwch Won Olwen* is a significant one. In that great epic, King Arthur's men must accomplish a series of tasks to ensure Culhwch can marry the woman he loves, Olwen. One of the more important tasks is hunting the Twrch Trwyth,[172] a giant boar who was laying waste to swathes of Ireland and Wales. The Twrch Trwyth was once the son of a chieftain, Taredd Wledig,[173] but was transformed into a giant boar as a punishment by God. That last part is a Christian interpretation of a much older concept found throughout the Celtic tradition: that humans can transform into animals.

The Twrch Trwyth is such a powerful agent of chaos, such a pure embodiment of the panic-driven wild, that only a very special hunter could ever bring him down. Your average mortal would wither and die by merely being brushed by one of his poisonous bristles. For this monster, you need one of those special hunters, someone like Mabon son of Modron ('Divine Son, son of Divine Mother'). If the great King Arthur and his men are to have a chance against the Twrch, then they will need to find Mabon. Unfortunately, he was taken from his mother's side when he was but three nights old, and no one has

---

171   MAB-on; 'ab' as in 'cab'. MOD-ron.

172   Twrch TRUE-ith.

173   TAR-eth Wl-ED-ig.

seen head or tail of him since. But Arthur's men are themselves a talented bunch, and may just have the skills to pull off such a seemingly impossible mission. The team includes one Gwrhyr Gwalstawd Ieithoedd[174] (Gwrhyr 'Interpreter of Languages'), a man who can talk to animals, and it just so happens that the best lead they have is to talk to some animals.

The animals who might know where Mabon is held captive are the oldest and wisest animals in the world. The first that Arthur's men visit is the Blackbird of Cilgwri.[175] When Gwrhyr asks if she knows the whereabouts of the lost Mabon, she says that she is so old she has worn a smith's anvil down to a nut by cleaning her beak against it every evening. Yet for all her years she knows nothing about Mabon.

But she knows of one who is older who may know, and she guides Gwrhyr and his companions to the Stag of Rhedynfre.[176] Gwrhyr asks him the same question, to which he responds he is so old he can remember when there were no trees in his forest except a single oak sapling that grew into a great tree. This fell and now nothing remains except for its stump. Yet for all his years, he knows nothing about Mabon. But he knows of one who is older who may know, and he guides Gwrhyr and his

---

174   GOOR-hir GWAL-stoud YAY-thoeth; 'oo' as in 'book' not 'soon'.

175   Ceel-GWR-i.

176   Rhed-IN-vre.

companions to the Owl of Cwm Cawlwyd.[177] Gwrhyr asks her where they can find Mabon, to which she responds she is so old she can remember when the valley they were in was a wooded glen, and men came and cut down the trees. Then a second forest grew and the wood they see now is the third. Yet for all her years, she knows nothing about Mabon. But she knows of one who is older who may know, and she guides Gwrhyr and his companions to the Eagle of Gwernabwy.[178] Gwrhyr asks him the same question, to which he responds:

> 'I came here in a distant time, and when I first came there was a rock here for me, and from its top I would peck the stars every evening. Now it's not a hand-breadth in height. Since then to this day I have been here, and I have heard nothing about the man you're asking about. Except once I went to seek my food as far as Llyn Lliw, and when I got there, I spread my claws into a salmon, thinking that he would be food for me for a long time, and he pulled me down into the depths, so that I almost failed to escape him. So what I and all my kinsmen did, was to attack him and try to destroy him. He sent messengers to make amends with me, and he came to me to have fifty tridents taken out of his back. Unless he knows something about what you are seeking, I do not know anyone who does. However, I shall be your guide to where he is.'[179]

---

177 COW-looid.

178 Gwer-NAB-ooi.

179 My translation of the text in Bromwich & Evans (1997), 32-3.

And of course, being the oldest animal in the world, the Salmon of Llyn Lliw[180] knows where Mabon is being held captive, and takes Arthur's men to him.

As with Gwion Bach's chase scene and the events preceding Dewi's conception, here we have a sequence of animals (three birds, a stag and a salmon) that correspond to the same three domains, again preceding the appearance of a wonder child. In *How Culhwch Won Olwen,* Mabon enters the story as a youth, but his captivity begins in infancy when he is three nights old. Although not a wonder child when he is rescued, his childhood and wondrous nature are significant parts of his story, never mind the fact that his name means 'Divine Son'. Mabon's discovery, like Taliesin's, is also connected to time and rivers: Mabon is held captive in a fortress on the banks of the River Severn that only the oldest and wisest animal — the salmon — has knowledge of, while the as-yet-unnamed Taliesin floats down a river and drifts for decades out on the Irish Sea.

The major difference between Taliesin's folktale and the stories of Dewi Sant and Mabon is that Gwion Bach becomes the animals, whereas in the other two tales the animals simply precede the hero. In this sense, Gwion Bach's transformations are perhaps more in keeping with those in the Irish story of Túan mac Cairell, preserved in the early twelfth-century manuscript known as *The Book of the Dun Cow.* Túan was a

---

180 Llin Lliw.

hermit that gave a welcome to an early missionary of the sixth century known as Finnian. While being hosted by his guest, Finnian beseeches Túan to tell him and his companions the history of Ireland, to which Túan reluctantly agrees.

He begins by recounting the arrival of the first people to Ireland, these being Greek settlers. After a plague wiped them out, only one survived, that being himself, Túan mac Cairell. Alone in the wilderness, he fled across the land, taking shelter from wolves in the high places and caves. He lived like a wild animal for thirty two years, in which time his hair and nails grew long and his body became shrivelled and wretched. It was then that his uncle landed in Ireland with a new company of Greek settlers, but he hid from them and remained alone.

Then one night while he slept, he dreamed he was transformed into a young stag, full of the joys of new life, leading a great herd across the land. During this time, he witnessed another group of settlers arrive, these being the people of Nemed who had suffered at sea, only three couples making it to the shores of Ireland. Yet they spread across the land and occupied the entire island before tragedy befell them all and they perished. Túan, by this time, was once again old and being pursued by men and wolves. Taking refuge in a cave, he fell asleep and dreamed that he transformed into a wild boar, once again happy in a new life as a leader of a herd of boars. Then another generation of settlers arrived, the Fir

Bolg, and by this time Túan was once again old and ready to change shape. After fasting for three days in the same cave, he transformed into a hawk and flew across Ireland, happy as ever, full of strength and learning all things. In the shape of a hawk, he witnessed the arrival of the 'tribes of gods and un-gods'. He was in that shape for a long time until he outlived all the people who had settled Ireland so far.

Then the sons of Míl conquered the island from the Tuatha Dé and Túan was so grief stricken that he fled to the hollow of a tree and there he fasted for nine nights, after which time he transformed into a river salmon and fled happily into a river where he was content, living as a vigorous and excellent swimmer that no fisher nor hawk could catch. Eventually, in his old age, he was caught in a net and taken to the wife of King Cairell. He was killed and cooked and the queen ate him so that he resided in her womb, and then he was born to her as a child. He grew to become a prophet, and he was named Túan. When he was old, St Patrick arrived with the Christian faith and he was baptised.[181]

Túan's story can be read as an origin story for Ireland, giving as it does an account of the different waves of settlers who came to the land. Yet that history was witnessed while Túan was in animal form, and just like the Welsh stories

---

181   A full translation can by found by John Carey, 'The Story of Túan son of Cairell' in *The Celtic Heroic Age* edited by John T. Koch (CSP 2013), 223-225.

outlined above, three different animals that correspond with the three natural domains of land, air and water. Like Mabon's story, the different animals appear to correspond to epochs of time, specifically memory of those epochs. Like Gwion Bach, he is also killed and then consumed by a woman who he thereby gets pregnant and is then born as her child. Perhaps just as significantly, like Taliesin, Túan is also born a prophet, his long history of reincarnation giving him a peculiar relationship to time.

All the tales we've looked at in this chapter use a sequence of animals to mark out a special character. They also use animals from the three domains, suggesting the whole Earth is being evoked through its different environs. Wild animals also appear to be expressions of a greater, supernatural reality that accompanies the human hero, becoming either his incarnations or signifying his birth or rescue. The Welsh bardic tradition cultivated a mythology about one of their founding fathers which, perhaps predictably, draws on a broader belief in how special souls turn up in the world. Even though there are significant differences between his tale and that of Túan, Mabon and Dewi, like them, Taliesin is marked out by wild nature, a theme that arises elsewhere in his myth.

'Kad Godeu' ('The Battle of the Trees') is perhaps the most famous poem from *The Book of Taliesin,* because of its inclusion in Robert Graves' influential book, *The White Goddess.* Unfortunately, his rendering of the poem is terribly flawed, and many of the theories that he builds on the back of his reconstruction make little sense. He claimed there was an ancient tree calendar encoded in this poem, but if there is one present, we are yet to find it. Graves was working with a rather bad English translation of the poem, which he then took apart by reordering the lines, terminally breaking the meaning of the Welsh original and further compounding the mess he was making.[182] This has become a bit of a red herring by today, and it's worth drawing a line under Graves' fantastical (though inspired) reworking of the poem so that we can better see how 'The Battle of the Trees' actually draws on Taliesin's myth.

The story of the battle itself is related in a few disconnected sections of the poem, but the major thrust of it appears to be a conflict between Gwydion, the Machiavellian magician of *The Fourth Branch of the Mabinogi*, against some unknown foe. *The Fourth Branch,* the last tale in the great eleventh-century epic of the *Mabinogi,* is itself a tale of magic and transformation, where Gwydion, one of the main characters, uses his supernatural power to trick and deceive others. Although not technically a

---

182   I discuss this in more detail in this video: https://celticsource.online/the-battle-of-the-trees-and-the-white-goddess/

court poet, in the *Mabinogi* story, he disguises himself as such to gain entry into royal strongholds where he uses his power of illusion to manipulate the nobles of the court. In *The Fourth Branch*, he is very much an immoral character whose intentions can never be trusted. 'The Battle of the Trees' gives a far more heroic portrayal of Gwydion, but he still possesses the same magic of transformation.

In a desperate moment of the battle, Gwydion calls on God's aid and is told to enchant an army of trees through the power of speech. In *The Fourth Branch*, Gwydion creates the illusion of dogs and horses and later on takes part in creating a woman of flowers. It's not clear why Gwydion is at war in the poem but according to a later story triad it was fought over 'a trifle: for three animals, a bitch, a roebuck and a curlew', all supposedly from the otherworld, Annwfn.

Again, this is in keeping with *The Fourth Branch* where Gwydion steals the magical pigs of Annwfn that had been gifted to the kingdom of Dyfed. But whereas the battle that resulted from that theft was fought in North Wales, 'The Battle of the Trees' was apparently fought at Caer Nefenhyr,[183] which may have been a historical stronghold in the Old North. As in all such traditions, the same characters and basic narratives can be reused in different contexts, giving rise to a diverse range of poems and stories that retain some similarities but also

---

183   Kire Nev-EN-hir; 'ire' as in 'ire'.

explore different situations and themes. Recycling elements of the tradition in this way breathes new life into old tales; those reused elements also show us which basic myths the storytellers and audiences gravitated to time and time again.

Taliesin appears to have been present in the battle, but his role is obscure. In some sections of the poem, he appears to have been one of the fighters, as we find in this couplet that comes at the end of a long description of the different trees taking part in the battle:

> The Oak's twigs ensnared us
>
> With *Gwarchan Maeldderw.*[184]

'Gwarchan Maeldderw'[185] is a very ambiguous poem copied into a fourteenth-century manuscript, but is almost certainly older by several centuries. *Gwarchan* means something like 'teaching poem', 'incantation' or, more generally, 'ancient, authoritative verse'.[186] It's referred to here as a famous bardic poem used by the oak as a type of incantation to ensnare 'us'. 'Us' probably refers to everybody taking part in the battle, which means the power summoned by the oak was indiscriminate, affecting

---

184 My translation of the text in Haycock (2015), 181.

185 GWARCH-an Mile-THERE-oo.

186 Kathryn A. Klar & Eve E. Sweetser, 'Reading the unreadable: Gwarchan Maelderw from the Book of Aneirin', in Kathryn A. Klar, Eve E. Sweetser & Claire Thomas (eds.), *A Celtic florilegium: studies in memory of Brendan O Hehir 2* (CSP 19960, 78–103.

the Cymry and their foe alike. Because the Welsh word for oak is *derw*,[187] and this is related to the Welsh word for druid, *derwydd*,[188] there may be a druidic subtext to this incantation-using oak. The oak is performing as if it were a magically powerful bard, often called a *derwydd*, 'druid' in the Welsh bardic tradition. If there is some symbolic code here, it is one where the trees are wizard-bards in conflict or competition. Was Taliesin one of a retinue engaged in magical warfare with an opposing troop of bards? The transformation from human bard to magical tree would be in keeping with the other transformations already discussed. We could also have this the wrong way around. Taliesin may have started out as a tree.

The idea of poetic power emanating from vegetative life is something Taliesin mentions again later on in the poem when discussing his own mysterious origins:

> I was not made
>
> By a mother and a father,
>
> And my creation was created for me
>
> From nine types of material. [189]

That is, Taliesin is not of human origin but was instead created

---

187 DARE-oo.

188 DARE-with.

189 My translation of the text in Haycock (2015), 181.

From fruit, from fruits,

From God's fruit at first,

From primroses and flowers,

From the blossom of trees and shrubs,

From earth, from sod

I was made,

From nettle blossom,

From the water of the ninth wave.

Math created me

Before I was finished.

Gwydion fashioned me

By the great enchantments of a magic wand.[190]

Once upon a time, before these poems were better understood, scholars believed this poem was a confused rag bag of different texts, and that this section was a poem in its own right, mistakenly copied into the midst of otherwise unrelated material. That poem was believed to describe the creation of a character called Blodeuedd[191] whose story is told, once again, in *The Fourth Branch of Mabinogi.* A rather unfortunate nobleman

---

190   Ibid. 181-2.

191   Blo-DAY-eth.

by the name of Lleu[192] has been cursed by his own mother never to wed a human wife. To circumvent the curse, Lleu's uncle, Gwydion the magician and Math the sorcerer-king of Gwynedd, work a great magic together:

> Then they took the flowers of the oak, and the flowers
> of the broom, and the flowers of the meadowsweet, and
> from those they conjured the fairest and most elegant
> maiden that anyone had ever seen. And they baptised her
> in their way, and gave Blodeuedd as her name.[193]

More recent scholarship now assumes this is one complete poem, so it's very unlikely this section is spoken by Blodeuedd, no matter how alike it is to her story. Instead, Taliesin appears to have been created similarly to the magical flower woman of *The Fourth Branch*, once again by the magic of Gwydion and Math. Taliesin is claiming that his origins are in growing wild vegetation, an idea echoed in the later folktale where Gwion Bach is transformed into a grain of wheat.

With *The Tale of Taliesin* in mind, we could also be looking at a list of ingredients to be brewed in a magic cauldron. Is Taliesin alluding to his origins in the potion of inspiration? In one sense, the ingredients of that potion are his symbolic parents, but that would make Math and Gwydion the potion brewers, not Ceridwen. The implication is that this is a different

192 Llay.

193 My translation of the text in Williams (1982), 83.

lineage in Taliesin's myth, where his origin story does not include the sorceress and her cauldron, but the enchantments of war-chiefs in the middle of a great, magical battle.

Either way, the implication in this section of the poem is that in one version of Taliesin's myth, his first transformation was into the form of a human. By claiming his parentage is in wild, green nature, he reveals himself to be a supernatural being who only came to be human through the enchantments of Gwydion and Math. To fit this into the story of 'The Battle of the Trees', he was fashioned on the occasion of a great battle that was to be fought with the power of magical speech, a war of incantatory fireworks fought by trees. What better origin story for the greatest wizard-bard of the Welsh nation? After a long sequence of past lives, in a later section of the poem Taliesin suddenly declares:

> My two keen spears
>
> Came from Heaven.
>
> In the streams of Annwfn
>
> They are made ready for battle.
>
> Eight thousand men
>
> I wounded, despite their ardour.[194]

---

194   My translation of the text in Haycock (2015), 183.

Was Taliesin conjured by Gwydion and Math as a weapon of great bardic destruction? If so, we must assume there is some logic and coherence to this obscure poem, and that it's not a rag bag of Taliesin stuff thoughtlessly thrown together. Despite this uncertainty, just like the trees and shrubs that took part in the battle, we can at least say that here, Taliesin is transformed green life drawing on the raw power of nature. In this sense, awen can be understood as an innate part of divine creation, if not the essence of the divine creative force itself, seen every springtime exploding in colourful and verdant beauty across the land. The fundamental act that's the source of creation is the same that's at the heart of all bardic endeavour, each created poem a microcosm of the sacred macrocosm.

Of all the transformations in Taliesin's myth, those that involve plants and animals draw on a theme that arises in several other Celtic myths: the wild, be that vegetation or animal, is a manifest expression of supernature. The mysterious powers of nature have been heard to speak with the voices of gods and goddesses in countless traditions across the world, so it's no real surprise to find these same divine voices speaking in Welsh myth. One such goddess hides in plain sight in *The Tale of Taliesin*, a goddess who not only confers the blessing of life transformed, but who also, by necessity, takes that life back.

CHAPTER 8

Ceridwen

... skilled and learned in the three arts, namely magic,

witchcraft and sorcery.

The earliest surviving reference to Ceridwen can be found in a poem composed sometime between 1100 and 1130 by one court bard in praise of another. The one being praised, Cuhelyn,[195] was a powerful nobleman in West Wales and was a good patron of the bardic arts he himself had been trained in. He almost certainly gave patronage to the anonymous poet who composed the following lines:

> Lord God, grant me overflowing awen
> (amen, let it be done),
>
> [Awen] of ardent song, abundant declamation,
> [like an] uproarious swarm,
>
> According to the honoured ode of Ceridwen,
> diverse ogrfen,
>
> Diverse riches, generous declamation
> for a skilful singer ...

---

195   Ki-HEL-in.

'Ceridwen's ode' is the classical craft of Welsh poetry, a tangible craft just like working wood or metal. It gave the bardic wordsmiths *ogrfen*, that being (as far as we can tell) one part or a division of awen. In this poem at least, it's a little easier to discern Ceridwen's relationship to the Christian God: she provides the container within which awen can be worked and formed. The original Welsh wording is *herwydd urdden awddl Cyrdifen*, and as well as meaning 'according to the honoured craft of Ceridwen' it also implies 'by virtue of the honoured craft', the subtle difference implying the practices she oversees are essential for the working of divine awen. Basically, it's not possible to work awen without her craft. This delineates precisely Ceridwen's role in the Welsh bardic tradition, at least for this anonymous bard.

But in the legendary poems from *The Book of Taliesin*, Ceridwen is not just the dignified mother of the classical craft of Welsh poetry, as we've already seen in 'The Hostile Confederacy', she is also described as an enemy:

> A hen received me
>
> A red-clawed one, a crested foe;
>
> I rested nine nights
>
> A child in her womb.[196]

---

196   My translation of the text in Haycock (2015), 122.

The bards had a complicated relationship with their symbolic mother; she inspired a *parchus ofn*[197] ('respectful fear'), as we say in Welsh. On the one hand, she brews the potion of awen from the plants and herbs of God-given creation, but to receive that gift the bard must submit to being consumed by her, perhaps so that she can kill off his immature and unrefined self. Only then can she restore him to a new life where he is endowed with her craft, a magical being able to work with the very power of divine creation.

'Rhithiadau Taliesin', 'Taliesin's Transformations', is a poem that can be dated to the fourteenth century, and comes from the broader tradition beyond *The Book of Taliesin*. It gives a very vivid portrayal of Ceridwen the great, enchanted huntress, once again in the voice of Taliesin:

> The first time I was fashioned,
> it was in the shape of a holy man;
>
> Hateful Ceridwen made me suffer.
>
> Even though I am small to look at,
> I always received a welcome [at court],
>
> I was great above the land, heaven guided me.
>
> I was a hostage within a body, sweet awen caused it to be;
>
> A trespasser without [his] people, easy to punish
>
> By the old, strong, black witch when she was angered.

---

197   PARCH-is ovn.

Terribly, she exercised her right when she attacked.[198]

It cannot be doubted that theirs was a love-hate relationship. This passage is the most explicit description we have of Taliesin's infancy in the dark witch's womb, a hateful condition akin to imprisonment. Even if the life itself is cherished, the experience of being born into countless forms is shot through with suffering and grief. There is a greater sense of desperation than what we find in the earlier legendary poems of the twelfth century, the usual bravado having fled with all the desperate animals. In the last section of the poem, after many transformations, Ceridwen catches her prey:

> On the edge of a winnowing-sheet I was caught.
>
> She was as large as a pregnant brood-mare
>
> Filling like a ship's sail upon the water.
>
> Into a dark belly I was spilled;
>
> From the sea tide, I was returned.
>
> A gift was given to me when I was well nurtured;
>
> Lord God easily released me.[199]

---

198 My translation of the text in Gruffydd (1997), 107.

199 Ibid.

The last couplet betrays the complex relationship between Taliesin and his mother-enemy. Ceridwen confers her gift of awen upon the infant bard while he is in her womb, a period of great nurturing that takes place before his divinely-appointed time is come.

These few lines are another succinct example of how Christian and pagan elements have been fused in this tradition. As we have already seen, Taliesin's shape-shifting is very much in keeping with the ancient theme of animal transformation in Celtic myth, and his death and rebirth through the *'strong, black witch'* has the flavour of folk belief and a far wilder sense of the supernatural. Yet this is all taking place within a Christian setting, where it is God who determines Taliesin's destiny, reinforcing the idea that for all of the pagan mysticism of his origin story, it is still a mysticism that the bards sought to harmonise with Christianity.

Elsewhere in mediaevel bardic poetry, we catch a few more glimpses of this powerful lady of the bardic craft. 'Kadeir Kerrituen', 'Ceridwen's Song', stands out from the other legendary poems in *The Book of Taliesin* as the only one composed in a woman's voice. The title includes an early rendering of Ceridwen's name, which in modern orthography gives us *Ceridfen*.[200] Although once believed to derive from the two syllables *cwrr* (meaning 'angular' or 'crooked') and *ben* (meaning 'woman'), Marged Haycock has pointed out that the meaning of the first part of her name is by no means settled. The old Celtic syllable *-ben* (here mutated to *-fen*), means 'woman' or 'female', as in the modern Welsh word *benyw*. But the first part *cerid-* (or *cyrid-* in earlier forms) could give a range of meanings including *Crytfen*: 'fever-' or 'shakes-woman', *Creidfen* 'passionate-' or 'inflamed-woman', and *Credidfen*: 'belief-' or 'faith-woman'.[201] All of these meanings bear on Ceridwen's character as she appears in *The Tale of Taliesin*, but because she is associated with cauldrons and potions, the mediaeval stereotype of the crooked witch is never too far away.

Much of 'Ceridwen's Song' deals with characters and events from *The Fourth Branch of the Mabinogi*, even though she herself doesn't appear in the version of the tale that has come down to us. This is significant because, as we shall see, even though she is absent from *The Fourth Branch* itself, her story in *The Tale of Taliesin* is similar to a few episodes in the *Mabinogi*. *The Fourth Branch* is concerned with the mythical family of Dôn who suffer because of the betrayals of Gwydion ap Dôn, the

---

200   Kur-ID-ven.

201   See Haycock (2015), 319-20.

powerful enchanter of 'The Battle of the Trees'. His disregard for the women of the court causes suffering and death.

'Ceridwen's Song' mentions events that are related to *The Fourth Branch*, but are not found elsewhere. After the standard greeting to the Christian God, Ceridwen says:

> Noble was the career of Miniog son of Lleu
>
> Whom I saw here not so long ago.[202]

Lleu is one of the main protagonists in *The Fourth Branch*, but he does not have a son in our version of the story. In fact, it's crucial to our *Fourth Branch* that he cannot become a father. This couplet at least sets the poem in the same imagined past as *The Four Branches,* a long-lost golden age where the Romans and Anglo-Saxons are yet to arrive in Britain. Ceridwen is speaking from an ancient past when the Brythonic tribes, the ancestors of the Welsh, still reigned supreme; this would be the Iron Age, historically speaking.

In the next couplet, Ceridwen tells us that Miniog's end *'was in the stony grave of Dinlleu,'* that is he was buried at Dinas Dinlle, an ancient Iron Age fortress overlooking Caernarfon Bay in north-western Wales. Dinlleu means 'Lleu's Fortress', his father's stronghold. Ceridwen is not only speaking from an

---

202   Ibid. 316.

ancient past, but from a place which is itself connected to *The Fourth Branch of the Mabinogi*. She goes on:

> Afagddu, my own son –
>
> Was made by gracious God.
>
> In poetic contests
>
> His sense was better than mine.

Afagddu is, of course, the other name for Morfran, Ceridwen's ugly son. He's portrayed here as an enlightened bard, implying there's some lost version of Ceridwen's story where he somehow gains the potion. Again, what we're seeing here is the natural diversity of an oral tradition, where different lineages and lore-keepers have developed a variety of narratives using common characters, motifs and symbols. Only some of these versions made it to manuscript, and only some of those manuscripts survived to our age.

This poem in particular comes from a lineage where both *The Fourth Branch* and *The Tale of Taliesin* were different from the versions we have. But that said, there are other parts of the poem that are the same as our version of *The Fourth Branch*. Particular mention is made of Gwydion's theft of pigs from the southern kingdom of Dyfed. He accomplished this by exchanging them for enchanted horses, saddles and shields, all of which turned out to be illusions that had disappeared by the next morning:

> The most skilful one I heard of
>
> Was Gwydion son of Dôn, always making splendid things,
>
> Who enchanted a woman from flowers,
>
> Who stole pigs from the South
>
> Because he had the best learning.
>
> He was bold in battle with cunning like
>
> The interlace of a chain,
>
> He created horses
>
> To overcome objections,
>
> And wondrous saddles.[203]

Again, as in 'Kad Godeu', Gwydion is heroic and worthy of praise, a different portrayal to the Machiavellian character that we find in the *Mabinogi*. Yet, there is one suggestion in Ceridwen's poem that Gwydion isn't always the praiseworthy enchanter she makes him out to be. In our *Fourth Branch*, we hear how he deceives his own sister, Arianrhod, when he creates the illusion of a great fleet attacking her island fortress:

---

203   Ibid. 316-7.

> Arianrhod, renowned for her beauty,
> surpassing the radiance of sunshine,
>
> Her terrifying was the greatest shame
> in the land of the Britons . . . [204]

Gwydion's terrorising of his own sister is a shameful act here, which agrees with his more negative portrayal in our *Fourth Branch*. Ceridwen has admiration for her fellow enchanter with just a touch of admonishment in this last section. This admiration may be because of her having a close relationship to Gwydion, doubtless a result of them both being respected figures at the court of Gwydion's mother, Dôn:

> When the songs are judged
>
> My own will be the best of them all:
>
> My song, my cauldron and my rules,
>
> And my careful declamation, a harmonious song.
>
> I'm known as a knowledgeable one in Dôn's court . . . [205]

Here again, we find that poetry is her craft: both the composition of poetry, that is *cerdd dafod* ('tongue craft'), and also the declamation of poetry, its performance during public ceremonies of praise, commemoration or bardic competition.

---

204 Ibid. 317-8.

205 Ibid. 317. Taliesin is also described breifly as one of Dôn's children in a Breton source. See the website for a discussion: https://celticsource.online/taliesin-origins

Regardless of how some of the poem's details diverge from other stories, this is the same Ceridwen that we find elsewhere, mother of the bardic tradition and lady of the craft of poetry.

'Ceridwen's Song' suggests she should be treated like other characters in the Welsh myths of the *Mabinogi*: she could have an ancient lineage in the oral traditions of the first millennium. Even though the only surviving story in which she plays a significant role was written down 450 years after *The Four Branches of the Mabinogi*, she clearly belongs to the same body of traditional lore. Her story can be read as a myth about a goddess, in her case a goddess of poetry not that dissimilar to other Indo-European figures such as Saraswati in the Vedic or Brigid in the Irish. We can at least discern an ancient lineage for this type of female character going back to the Celtic Iron Age. In a first-century description of Celtic priestesses by the Roman geographer Pomponius Mela, we find a coven of spiritually potent women who could easily be Ceridwen's ancestors:

> *Sena, in the Britannic Sea, opposite the coast of the Osismi, is famous for its oracle of a Gaulish god, whose priestesses, living in the holiness of perpetual virginity, are said to be nine in number. They call them Gallizenae,*

and they believe them to be endowed with extraordinary
gifts to rouse the sea and the wind by their incantations,
to turn themselves into whatsoever animal form they
may choose, to cure diseases which among others are
incurable, to know what is to come and to foretell it. They
are, however, devoted to the service of voyagers only who
have set out on no other errand than to consult them.[206]

Such women dedicated to a spiritual craft, particularly those endowed with the power of animal transformation, appear to have a long tradition in Celtic culture. We can take this a step further and guess at Ceridwen's mythology as a goddess in her own right by seeing how her tale compares with other similar myths. As discussed earlier, she's related to characters and events in *The Fourth Branch of the Mabinogi*, even though she herself doesn't play a part that story. One episode in particular shares some intriguing similarities with *The Tale of Taliesin*, that being the climax of *The Fourth Branch* where the young nobleman, Lleu is killed and then resurrected.

Lleu's mother, Arianrhod, swears a great destiny upon him that he shall never have a human wife. To circumvent such a difficult destiny, his uncle, Gwydion, seeks the aid of the sorcerer-king, Math, and they both set about conjuring a bride of flowers. With great magic they create Blodeuedd, ('Flowers') and give her as a wife to Lleu. Alas, she will not abide by the

---

206   Pomponius Mela, *De Chorographia* iii, chap. 6, translated by Gustav Parthey, (GADV 1969), 72.

marriage, taking another nobleman, Gronw Pebr, as her lover and scheming with him to do away with Lleu. They kill him with a cursed spear. At the moment of his death, Lleu takes flight as an eagle and disappears.

After searching long through the land, Gwydion hears of a sow that's been behaving strangely. He asks the swineherd to release the sow, and she takes off with Gwydion in hot pursuit. He catches up to her at an otherworldly oak tree, beneath which she is foraging rotten flesh and maggots that are falling from somewhere up in the tree.

When Gwydion looks up, he sees a rotten eagle perched on the top branch. Gwydion sings a short incantation to the eagle, and it descends to the middle of the tree. Then he sings another, and it descends to the bottom branch. After a third incantation, the eagle lands in his lap, where he strikes it with his magic wand and turns it back into the form of Lleu, emaciated and still suffering from the wound made by the cursed spear. Gwydion heals Lleu, and they exact their revenge on both Blodeuedd and Gronw Pebr. Lleu kills Gronw in the manner in which the latter had killed him and Gwydion transforms Blodeuedd into an owl. But in the end, Arianrhod's final destiny has not been circumvented, and the tale ends with Lleu ascending to the throne of Gwynedd but unable to take a wife or produce an heir.

Although not immediately apparent, Lleu's story bears some similarity to *The Tale of Taliesin*. Both Gwydion and Ceridwen are sorcerers, powerful magic users well versed in transforming their own shapes and those of others. Ceridwen's connection to the bardic arts should be obvious by now; likewise Gwydion is described in the *Mabinogi* as 'the best storyteller in the world' and uses incantatory verse to sing Lleu down from the magic oak tree.

Beyond these background details, we find that both Gwydion and Ceridwen are implicated in the deaths of their respective 'quarries'. Gwydion is directly responsible for the situation that results in Lleu's murder by the flower-woman, Blodeuedd; Ceridwen simply eats Gwion. Both sorcerers are involved in an animal pursuit across the land: Gwydion pursues both the Lleu-eagle and the sow, whereas Ceridwen hunts the Gwion-animal through his several transformations. Perhaps more significantly, both pursuits are connected to the transcendence of death: Lleu dies, his soul fleeing as an eagle and is then resurrected by Gwydion; Gwion Bach flees for his life, is caught, killed, and reincarnated through Ceridwen.

We also have two members of the senior generation having a life-transforming effect on the lives of their juniors: in Ceridwen's case, that of her actual child and in that of Gwydion, the life of his nephew and foster-son. The basic narrative that's revealed when we compare both stories looks something like this:

1. A sorcerer connected to the bardic arts

2. pursues the animal-transformed soul of their child across a landscape,

3. who dies and then transcends death

4. because of the actions of the sorcerer,

5. and goes on to live a second life.

The presence of this same basic structure in both tales raises some questions, perhaps the most obvious being: can we consider this a basic type of myth? It certainly qualifies if by myth we mean an old story, but beyond that it also deals with a common theme in mythologies across the world, that of rebirth. The continuation of life after death is perhaps one of the most common religious themes in human culture, and belief in that continuity has been a matter of faith for tens of thousands of years if the evidence of ancient burial practices is anything to go by.[207] It's easy to see in this basic narrative the myth of a parental deity instigating transformation, death and rebirth. Like many other deities, they are responsible for the entire cycle of human existence.

---

207   For example, a 78,000 year old human burial has been discovered in Africa. See Maria Martinón-Torres et al, 'Earliest known human burial in Africa', *Nature*, 5.5.2021.

A significant difference is that one version features a male sorcerer while the other a female, and we can distinguish a different type of rebirth enacted by both. Gwydion brings about a resurrection for Lleu, and in that we could follow a Christian comparison, especially considering how the episode features a supernatural tree: a common symbol for Christ's cross. Conversely, Ceridwen causes Gwion Bach's reincarnation as Taliesin, with the animal transformations perhaps standing for other incarnations in the intervening period, a distinctly pagan type of rebirth.

This could also be seen as a god who enacts resurrection replacing a goddess who enacts rebirth through biological gestation.[208] It's not possible to discern what cultural influences led to these variations, but we can at least see that the basic narrative they draw upon contains mythological themes that persisted in the broader Celtic culture of mediaevel Europe.[209] Yet even though it would be reasonable to assume this basic narrative is older than both of its variations, it's impossible to

---

208   With thanks to Simon H. Lilly for pointing this out.

209   For example, in his paper 'The Old Gods of Ireland in the Later Middle Ages', John Carey discusses a comparable feature of Irish culture: ' . . . it is clear enough that the nature of the old gods, and their relationship with ideas concerning the realm of the dead and perhaps some kind of reincarnation, were living issues in the Ireland of the High and later Middle Ages. It was not merely a matter of survivals among the peasantry; if it had been, the erudite elite who held the monopoly on writing would simply have ignored such notions, or at best made them the subject of a few contemptuous allusions. No: these are questions which were taken seriously by men of learning. The people of the *Side* were still there, and still claimed some power over the souls of mortals.' in *Understanding Celtic Religion* (UWP 2015), Katja Ritari & Alexandra Bergholm (eds.).

say how old. At least the few clues we have — the presence of druid-like sorcerers, animal transformation and reincarnation — all point to a pagan origin, perhaps even a pre-Christian one.

There are other basic similarities between *The Tale of Taliesin* and episodes in *The Four Branches of the Mabinogi*. In the poem 'Golychaf-i Gulwydd' ('I Petition God'), Taliesin claims:

> I sang at a feast over a cheerless drink,
>
> I sang before the sons of Llŷr in the estuaries of Henfelen; . . .[210]

Here, Taliesin is talking about the part he plays in *The Second Branch*, where he is one of the seven companions that spend decades being feasted by the severed head of the giant Bendigeidfran.[211] *The Second Branch* is the tragic tale of Branwen, given in marriage to Matholwch,[212] the king of Ireland. Bendigeidfran, Branwen's brother and king of Britain, has arranged her marriage to Matholwch to ensure peace between the two nations; Branwen dutifully submits

---

210 My translation of the text in Haycock (2015), 275.

211 Bendy-GAYD-vran.

212 Math-OL-ooch; 'oo' as in 'book'.

herself to this politically convenient union. Unfortunately for all concerned, Branwen's half-brother, Efnysien,[213] was not consulted on the union, and in a petulant rage maims the Irish king's horses during the wedding celebrations. Then, on returning with Matholwch to Ireland, Branwen finds that the Irish courtiers have not forgiven the Welsh for Efnysien's insult and they demand that she be punished in revenge. Matholwch bows to this pressure and sends Branwen, his new queen, to work in the kitchens where the butcher beats her every day. Yet the Irish court realise that their mistreatment of Branwen must never come to the attention of her giant brother, Bendigeidfran, out of fear of his wrath.

Meanwhile, Branwen finds friendship in a starling that comes to sit every day on the edge of her kneading trough. She teaches it to speak and tells it to take a message to her brother Bendigeidfran, telling him of her captivity and mistreatment. The starling flies across the Irish Sea and delivers the message, stirring the Welsh into action. Bendigeidfran crosses to Ireland with a large host. After pursuing the Irish, he corners them and forces them to negotiate: it is agreed that Matholwch should relinquish his throne to his and Branwen's son, Gwern.[214] But Efnysien, the psychotic brother, is dissatisfied with the arrangement, and on the pretence of embracing his nephew,

---

213 Ev-NUS-yen.

214 Gwairn.

Gwern, he throws the boy into a fire and kills him. In the following uproar there is carnage and bloodshed, and although the Welsh overcome the Irish in a great battle, Bendigeidfran is mortally wounded in the foot with a poisoned spear. In this sorry condition, Bendigeidfran commands the seven surviving companions, Taliesin amongst them, to cut off his head and take it back to London to bury it under the Gwynfryn,[215] a blessed hill, where it will serve as a talisman of protection for the whole island. But before that burial, he tells them they will be feasted and entertained for several magical decades.

On their return home with Bendigeidfran's head, Branwen dies of a broken heart and is buried close to the River Alaw in Môn. From there the seven companions take Bendigeidfran's severed head to Harlech[216] on the west coast of Wales, where they are feasted for seven years, the head continuing to speak to them in its undead state. Then they travel to the island of Gwales[217] off the Welsh coast, where they are feasted this time for eighty years, the head again speaking to them, entertaining them as well as Bendigeidfran ever did when he was alive. While in Gwales, none of the companions age and neither do they feel the grief of the tragic war in Ireland; they are in an otherworldly time-out-of-time where only the joys of the

---

215 GWIN-vrin.

216 HAR-lech.

217 GWAL-es; 'al' as in 'shall'.

moment are present to them. When the timeless feast ends, the seven companions return to the temporal realm, their grief and suffering flooding back as mortality takes hold once more. They travel to London where they eventually lay the giant's head to rest, and he speaks no more.

Hidden in this summary of *The Second Branch* is the shape of another old story, and to bring it to light, we must draw a comparison with Lleu's tale in *The Fourth Branch*. The first similarity is that of Lleu and Bendigeidfran themselves: both have identities connected to birds. In *The Fourth Branch*, Lleu's fate is entwined with that of a little wren. Lleu's mother, Arianrhod, is tricked into giving him his name when she sees him cast a needle at a wren, skilfully striking the bird in the leg between the tendon and the bone. This naming of Lleu is his symbolic birth into personhood; before this, he is nameless and bereft of identity. This rather cruel game is revisited upon Lleu at his own death, when his enemy, Gronw Pebr, strikes him with a spear, and at the very moment of his death Lleu transforms into a wounded eagle, an echo of the wren and a symbolic description of his own soul in transmigratory flight. At the symbolic beginning and end of Lleu's life, we find birds.

Likewise, Bendigeidfran's identity seems to be bound to crows: his name means 'blessed crow' (*bendigaid* + *brân*). His fate is also determined by the actions of his sister, Branwen, whose name is the feminine version of his own (*brân* + *gwen* =

'crow' + 'white' / 'blessed'). She makes her desperate plea for rescue through a starling, an act that brings about her brother's death.

Where there are two bird-men in *The Second* and *Fourth Branches*, there are also two bird-women. We've already seen how Branwen is connected to birds, and in *The Fourth Branch* Blodeuedd, Lleu's wife, is transformed into an owl by Gwydion as a punishment for her role in Lleu's murder. This is also the moment Gwydion gives her a new name, Blodeuwedd,[218] 'Flower Face', a metaphorical description of an owl's face. If we bring Ceridwen into the equation, we see that each woman can be identified with a bird, and animals in general in Ceridwen's case.

To take this further, all three women are wronged by their counterparts: Branwen submits to her brother's will and agrees to an arranged marriage that turns out to be abusive and ultimately the cause of her death; Blodeuedd was given to Lleu without her consent in an arranged marriage that she seeks to escape by killing him; Ceridwen believes Gwion Bach stole the priceless potion of awen from her. Because of being wronged, unwittingly or otherwise, these women bring about the deaths of the males who wronged them: Branwen, though innocent of any malicious intent, is the reason Bendigeidfran is drawn into his disastrous, final war and killed by poisoned

---

218   Blod-AY-weth.

spear; Blodeuedd plans and aids in Lleu's murder with a cursed spear; Ceridwen eats Gwion.

But perhaps more significantly, each of these three males do not die in the way we would expect them to. Each one transcends death: Bendigeidfran's severed head entertains the seven companions in the otherworldly time-out-of-time; Lleu flees to the magic oak tree as an eagle and is then resurrected; Gwion Bach is eaten by Ceridwen, but nine months later is reborn. What's more, a special type of speech is connected to the deaths of each of these male characters: Bendigeidfran continues to speak even though he should be dead; Lleu is resurrected through Gwydion's use of incantatory verse; Gwion Bach's reincarnation as Taliesin sees him becoming the greatest conjurer of words in the Welsh tradition. In simple terms, all three stories follow the same pattern:

1. A woman who has an animal identity

2. is wronged by a male

3. who likewise has an animal identity.

4. As a consequence, the male is killed,

5. either directly or indirectly by the actions of the woman,

6. but the male somehow transcends his death,

7. and that transcendence involves magical speech.

The stories of Branwen and Bendigeidfran, Blodeuedd and Lleu, Ceridwen and Gwion Bach all follow this same basic sequence, but in unique ways. It looks like a myth preserved like a fossil in the strata of the later tales, a myth about the transcendence of death. The animal identities of the two protagonists are an ancient theme that can be traced back to the shape-shifting figures of the Celtic Iron Age. They are magical identities, ritualised figures engaged in a process of transformation through death, and the incantatory use of language lends a further ritual quality to the story.

What's so striking about this pattern is how consistent it is even though it's expressed so differently in each story. The climax of the sequence, the transcendence of death, is as profound in each version, yet it's accomplished in very unique ways: Bendigeidfran is in a liminal, undead state for a long time before succumbing fully to death; Lleu dies, transforms and is resurrected; it's only in Ceridwen's story we find an explicit description of reincarnation involving a magical mother figure. Many of the storytellers that had a hand in the development of these stories adhered to the theme of transcended death regardless of how different their own versions had become. The basic myth — and perhaps the belief it expresses — remained coherent for a long period. How long we shall never know, but long enough for it to be preserved in three different versions in the Welsh tradition.

Here we have another underlying pattern that connects both *The Tale of Taliesin* and *The Four Branches of the Mabinogi*. The first similarity between Ceridwen and Gwydion and the second between her, Branwen and Blodeuedd, compound many of the themes already discussed. The two patterns are like different root networks sharing the same soil. Ceridwen's role in the transformation, death and rebirth of her own child, bound up as it is with these other old stories, reveals her myth to be amongst the oldest preserved in Welsh culture.

Ceridwen's story is drawn from a branch of Celtic myth that explores magical identities, transformation, the transcendence of death and magical speech. In *The Tale of Taliesin*, although it's Gwion Bach who experiences these things, they are brought about by Ceridwen. If her myth contains a spiritual philosophy (as old myths tend to), Ceridwen embodies a natural law: death gives rise to new life; destruction is the precursor to creation. She is the Great Destroyer and Great Mother, a role she accomplishes with great economy, destroying Gwion Bach in the very moment she impregnates herself with his seed.

Yet Ceridwen accomplishes more than a turning of the life-death cycle through her own body. She also provides the potion of awen that is both the instigator of change and the source of timeless awareness. Her concoction not only gives Gwion Bach the ability to *see* beyond time, but also the ability to *move* beyond time: he survives death with his memory and magical enlightenment intact. It is a condition unaffected by death. Other traditions preserve similar ideas, such as that of the Tibetan *lama*: a spiritual master experiences birth, life, death and then rebirth.[219] The soul and its memory are durable while the body changes and transforms.

Ceridwen's myth contains the two basic principles of change and permanence, and the spiritual philosophy that emerges also appears to describe her bards seeking to preserve their own essence through their tradition, transmitting it beyond each generation's death. Likewise, with the legendary Taliesin, his form is forever changing through countless objects, animals, and phenomena, yet he's one singular and unchanging personality who experiences these transformations. Taliesin is permanence in change, a blessing conferred upon him by Ceridwen.

For all of her potency as a goddess of transformation and memory, Ceridwen's status would never be secure in the broader, patriarchal, and often misogynistic culture of mediaevel Wales. Whereas the court bards of the eleventh, twelfth and thirteenth centuries paid her dues, as the millennium wore on, more and

219   Specifically a *sprulku lama*.

more set her aside, until the only place she retained her full, mythic potential appears to be in the common culture of the folk and their stories. By the fourteenth and fifteenth centuries, her magic cauldron, magic potions, powerful sorcery, and animal transformations, all gave her away as a stereotypical witch.

Today, witchcraft can be considered a type of religion, but this wasn't necessarily the case in Renaissance Europe. There was a substantial culture of common practices and mysticism, but witchcraft included so many diverse cultural elements throughout the Europe of this period that it's difficult to see it as an organised religion. There was no centralised authority that set out dogma or sought to control relations between witches. It was a far more anarchic culture, and even though there were shared beliefs, it included a diverse range of practices involving herbalism, mystic visions and countless ways of casting spells. It was also a very maligned and misunderstood part of folk culture. Nachman Ben-Yehuda describes the situation in the early Renaissance:

> . . . witchcraft was regarded as a routine, day-to-day (almost personal) technology until the fourteenth century; witches were classified as good or bad, depending on the objective of their magic. After the fourteenth century, a whole systematic theory was devoted to witchcraft: books were written on the subject, and experts specialised in its theory ("demonologists") and practice ("inquisitors,"

"witch-hunters," and the like). This analytical shift to the "new" eclectic demonological theories was precisely what was needed to enable the inquisitors, and other individuals, to persecute legitimately hundreds of thousands of witches.[220]

The study of witchcraft became a scholarly pursuit among the upper classes, and most significantly became a way of justifying the persecution of parts of the lower class, largely women, who were deemed to live outside the social norms of the Christian mainstream. Using the skills they had been taught at university and egged on by a militant Church, hobbyist scholars devoted their leisure time to the study of these exotic creatures. Some have even speculated whether the obsessive writings of the Renaissance *literati* tells us more about their paranoia than it does about the beliefs and practices of witchcraft itself.[221] Far from bringing about greater enlightenment and understanding, the universities of mediaeval and early modern Europe facilitated an attack on the powerless by the powerful, developing alongside the Church an entire structure of persecution. It's in these circumstances that the stereotype of The Witch develops in the popular imagination of Europe, where the different folk-magic practitioners were studied as a single category. These often

---

220   Nachman Ben-Yehuda, 'The European Witch Craze of the 14th to 17th Centuries: A Sociologist's Perspective', *American Journal of Sociology* Vol. 86, No. 1 (1980).

221   See John O. Ward, 'Magic and Rhetoric From Antiquity to the Renaissance: Some Ruminations', *Rhetorica: A Journal of the History of Rhetoric* Vol. 6, No. 1 (1988), 111.

fantastical descriptions all merged into the rather cartoonish figure of a flawed, sub-human creature used to whip up the murderous moral panics of the trials and burnings.

We find this stereotype in Shakespeare's *Macbeth*, where the three weird sisters chant their spells over a bubbling cauldron. A significant influence on Shakespeare was a book called *Demonologie*, written in 1597 by no less than King James I of England, a typical thesis on witchcraft as conjured in the minds of the paranoid elite. King James is just one example from the European ruling class who saw witchcraft as a threat to the fabric of society. His book, amongst many others, was part of a long-running campaign of persecution against peasant folk, the simple lie being that their spiritual culture was a danger to Christian civilisation. This was the justification for the prosecution of the witch trials and the legitimising of mob violence against some of the weakest and most disenfranchised members of society. Estimates of the number of witches murdered between 1400 and 1782 range from 40,000 to 60,000.[222]

In the middle of this witch craze, Elis Gruffydd and John Jones wrote their respective versions of *The Tale of Taliesin*, Gruffydd in the 1540s and Jones in 1607. In keeping with the broader Taliesin tradition, the Ceridwen of their versions is a figure to be feared. But in both accounts, her depiction is not

---

222   See Brian P. Levack, *The Witch Hunt in Early Modern Europe* (Routledge 2016).

as cartoonish as the stereotype of the European mainstream. She is a learned woman, a mistress of the Virgilian arts (magic as imagined by Renaissance scholars), someone who has an awareness of social status and who wants to do the best for her children. She's different from the three sisters in Shakespeare's *Macbeth*. Ceridwen isn't a malevolent monster, but a powerful noblewoman in her own right, erudite and skilled.

Some note that the persecution of witches wasn't as extreme in Wales as it was elsewhere in Europe.[223] There certainly was persecution and plenty of negative folk tales about this or that witch and the fate that befalls her. But the moral panic wasn't as fervent in Wales as it was elsewhere. Did the high regard given to the most famous Welsh witch of them all, Ceridwen, dampen witch paranoia in Welsh society? It's impossible to say for certain, but our history suggests there was a different attitude to folk magic in Wales.

That said, as Kristopher Hughes discusses in his book *Cerridwen*,[224] the tide was turning in the Welsh bardic tradition, and the dogmatic attacks of the clergy likely pressured the bards to ditch their more heretical beliefs. It's in this context that we see some court bards diverging from the traditional vision of Ceridwen as an honourable (if scary) patron of the bardic craft.

---

223 See Sally Parkin, 'Witchcraft, Women's Honour and Customary Law in Early Modern Wales', *Social History* Vol. 31, No. 3 (August 2006), 295-318.

224 (Llewellyn 2021), 76-7.

Iolo Goch was one of the most prominent praise poets of the late fourteenth century, and composed for the entertainment of the nobility. The attitudes we find in his poetry can be considered common to that class, at least within his particular social circles (including such luminaries as Owain Glyndŵr). Although not shared by all Welsh folk, Iolo Goch's attitudes show how the times were changing. In a long, satirical eulogy, he pokes fun at the passing of a cartoonish old woman by the name of Hersdin Hogl ('Hovel Rump'), with lines such as the following:

> She alleged that she had lived long
>
> In the time of old Ceridwen;
>
> Ostentatious and wanton woman, I know of her lust,
>
> Biggest sow, wrinkle-thumbed, food-crab,
>
> Unpleasant, twice-scabbed battering-ram, . . .
>
> In her apron, scram-demanding old witch,
>
> She went to the burial, cage of the aged.
>
> Foolish cow, never was there above her head
>
> Any manner of holy mass to be had.[225]

---

225 My translation of the text in Dafydd Johnston (ed.), *Gwaith Iolo Goch* (UWP 1988), 162.

Such attitudes amongst the nobility may not have permeated the common culture of the folk where old women lived and worked in poverty, sometimes as midwives and herbalists. Yet the snide portrayal of such a cartoonish witch by the upper classes may well have been a reflection of some broader attitudes. Although not a direct attack on Ceridwen, it was aimed at women of her 'type', and was part of a trend that saw less prominence for the noble Ceridwen. This slow but certain decline in her reputation was also a sign of how the mythology she embodied was waning. We can guess that as the dawn of the modern era arrived, fewer and fewer communities would have told her tale. By the time we reach the industrial revolution, only a few vestiges of her myth appear in the folktales of the eighteenth and nineteenth centuries.

One of the latest examples of Taliesin's story is preserved in the letters of Lewis Morris, an Anglesey poet and scholar of the eighteenth century. In his very brief version, Ceridwen has been replaced by two *gwiddan,* an old term that's often translated as 'witch' but in fact may be related to the words *gwŷdd,* 'tree'; *gŵydd,* 'wild'; or even the stem *gwŷdd-,* 'knowledge'.

> *[Taliesin] being a poor boy begging his bread: came by chance to Creigiau'r Eryri where there were two Gwiddans Boyling a Panfull of Enchanted Liquor: which they could not bring to perfection for want of fuell: Taliesyn asked them if he should boyl ye liquor. And told them that he had a particular way to make much water*

boil with little fuell: which they easily granted. Taliesyn
gathered ye fuell together and bound it in little fagotts
and so in a little time (and before they were aware of him)
he boyled ye liquor to perfection: and took ye first drops
to himself — The virtue of ye water was such that He that
had ye first 3 drops of it when boyled... should properly
be inspired with ye spirit of divining and this water
the Gwiddan's intended to give to their own sons (and
Taliesyn having heard of it,) he Endeavoured to make his
Escape but was caught by ym and cast into ye sea in a
Leather Bagg.[226]

Even though some main features are missing, it shows that in the common culture at least, the story persisted. It also preserves the basic theme that an average boy, here poor and perhaps orphaned, only requires the first three drops of a witches' brew to become an enlightened poet. The crucial role of the common herbalist's potion in the transformation of the boy says as much about the power of these women as it does about the origins of Taliesin. Ceridwen may not have been named in this late telling of the tale, but her shadow looms large in the background.

Even though the earliest surviving version of *The Tale of Taliesin* is from the middle of the sixteenth century, the tradition concerning the mythic figure that became Ceridwen was ancient by that time. Even though she eventually falls foul of the same paranoia and misogyny that destroyed the lives of

---

226   Lewis Morris, Cwrtmawr 14.10. (1726).

tens of thousands of witches, during the preceding centuries her myth expressed a potent spiritual philosophy. The concepts and themes that she embodies are to be found in cultures and traditions across the world, where they are more readilly acknowledged as part of the religious thinking of humanity.

CHAPTER 9

Annwfn

... he wandered from the time of Arthur to about the beginning of Maelgwn's, which was about forty years.

More often than not, Annwfn[227] is said to be the Welsh 'otherworld'. It isn't the worst description, but neither is it the most accurate.[228] An 'other' world can evoke the idea of a distant realm, far removed from our own, whereas Annwfn appears to be a little closer. The name Annwfn (sometimes spelled more colloquially 'Annwn') comprises two parts: *an-* is often read as the preposition 'in', or in this context 'inside' or 'inner';[229] *dwfn* (here mutated according to Welsh grammar to *-nwfn*) is a noun that has a few meanings in Middle Welsh: 'world' or 'sea'; but also as in Modern Welsh 'deep' and

---

227 AN-oovn; 'oo' as in 'book'.

228 See P. Sims-Williams, *Irish Influence on Mediaevel Welsh Literature* (OUP 2011), 53-6.

229 See P. Sims-Williams, 'Some Celtic Otherworld Terms' in Celtic Languages, Celtic Cultures edited by A.T.E Matonis & Daniel F. Medina (California 1990), 62.

'profound.' Altogether, Annwfn can be read as meaning 'inner world' or 'inner depth' with connotations of profundity.

Before we delve too deep, I'd like to stress that we should be wary of ascribing a modern Jungian meaning to Annwfn as representing the unconscious (collective or otherwise). This can obscure the nuances of the traditional concept of a world-within-the-world, as opposed to a facet of psychology. Jungian interpretations can be useful and interesting but they often tell us more about modern thinking than that of the past. There are a few reasons why we should avoid thinking about Annwfn as simply being something inside our heads.

In Welsh folklore we find it's often described as a subterranean realm. For Dafydd ap Gwilym, one of the greatest bards of the fourteenth century, it's the place the sun goes during winter. In his 'Praise of Summer', the sun says '*I Annwfn o ddwfn ydd af*',[230] 'To Annwfn from the world I will go', implying Annwfn is not of this world, yet adjacent to it. Elsewhere in Dafydd ap Gwilym's poems, it's the place a fox makes its home: '*A'i dŷ annedd hyd Annwn*', 'And his dwelling place as far as Annwn', meaning deep down in a hole.[231] In a mythological sense, this suggests an underworld below ground, which may have been part of its meaning deep in the Celtic

---

230 My translation of the text in Dafydd Jonhston et al (eds.), *Cerddi Dafydd ap Gwilym* (UWP 2010), 154. Notice *dwfn* is used here in its other sense as 'the world'.

231 Ibid. 230.

past.[232] There is no sign it was ever considered a facet of our psychology, but rather something independent.

The most detailed description of Annwfn in mediaevel literature, and perhaps the earliest to have survived, can be found in *The First Branch of the Mabinogi*, where Pwyll, the prince of Dyfed, is taken to the magical realm by its king, Arawn. The journey there doesn't appear to be that difficult, it simply requires Arawn's guidance:

> 'Your way will be unhindered, and nothing will delay you
> until you get to my land, and I will guide you.' [Arawn]
> guided him until he saw the court and dwelling-places.[233]

While in Annwfn, Pwyll does good deeds that reveal his virtue, as if being in this deeper realm empowers him to act according to the heroic ideal. In this sense, Annwfn is a realm of perfection in *The Four Branches of the Mabinogi*. It also appears to be close to the mortal realm, not underground, but simply imminent in certain places.

Elsewhere in *The Four Branches*, we find other spaces that, although not explicitly called Annwfn, share many of its qualities. The time-out-of-time in which Bendigeidfran's severed head feasts the seven companions, and the oak tree where the Lleu-eagle is found by Gwydion are both suggestive

232 See Sims-Williams (2011), 58.

233 My translation of the text in Ifor Williams (ed.) *Pedeir Keinc y Mabinogi* (UWP 1982), 3.

of somewhere other than the temporal realm of mortals. It's more of a place that's close-by, a dimension adjacent to our own, perhaps simply a deepening of it.

By comparison, we can also see how the infant Taliesin's time out at sea, floating around in his skin bag for forty years, is where Annwfn appears in Gruffydd's version of the folktale. This is a liminal period of decades where a mortal being would have naturally perished, never mind fail to grow at all; being washed ashore can likewise be understood as a return to the realm of the living. We shall explore the further implications of this episode in the next chapter, but for the time being, we can see how it corresponds to the Annwfn-like places in the other stories we've looked at. Taken together, the mediaevel understanding of Annwfn was not as a chthonic underworld, but this was perhaps a metaphorical description of a world-within-the-world, a depth that is everywhere.

Of course, these affirmative descriptions of Annwfn would have been an issue for the more dogmatic Christians of mediaevel Wales. A native otherworld where the souls of the dead flee as eagles or where young noblemen come to embody perfected ideals simply doesn't fit into the Christian view of the world. One sign of this is a rather awkward mention of the Welsh otherworld in *How Culhwch Won Olwen,* where we find this description of Gwyn ap Nudd,[234] another name for the king of Annwfn in Welsh folklore:

> '. . . *God put the nature of Annwfn's devils in him, lest the world be destroyed. He will not be spared from there.*'[235]

This is one of the earliest descriptions of Annwfn as the Christian hell. Gwyn ap Nudd not only embodies the nature of Annwfn but neither will God allow him to leave, suggesting Annwfn is both within him and also the place he resides in. Even though this is in direct contrast to *The Four Branches of the Mabinogi,* over the following centuries, Annwfn becomes more and more fixed in its Christian depiction and is treated far less as an indigenous otherworld. The native concept never fully disappears, but it's absorbed further into the Christian mainstream until, by today's modern Welsh culture, Annwfn is commonly synonymous with *uffern,*[236] simply 'hell'.

The earliest mention of Annwfn to have survived in poetry is in the work of Cynddelw Brydydd Mawr,[237] easily the greatest

---

234 Gwyn ap Neeth.

235 My translation of the text in Bromwich & Evans (1997), 27.

236 IF-ern.

237 Kun-THE-lw BRUD-ith Mour; 'mou' as in 'mouse'.

court bard of the twelfth century. Before Cynddelw, there is
a suggestion of the otherworld in a few rare places, but it's
not mentioned in the work of the historical Taliesin, that of
his contemporary Aneirin, nor in the early Welsh saga poetry,
more commonly known as the period of the *Cynfeirdd*[238] ('Early
Bards') that runs up to 1100 CE.

The following period, that of the *Gogynfeirdd*[239] ('Not-
So-Early Bards'), includes the work of Cynddelw, Llywarch ap
Llywelyn, most of the legendary poems in *The Book of Taliesin,*
and all other poetry up to 1300 CE. Then comes the period
of the Poets of the *Uchelwyr*[240] ('the Nobility'), poets such as
Dafydd ap Gwilym and Rhys Goch Eryri, who maintained
the Welsh bardic tradition after Wales lost its independence
in 1282. Throughout all three periods, there are only a few
mentions of Annwfn in its native sense: in poetry, the majority
are in the *Gogynfeirdd* period, tending towards the turn of the
twelfth century, and the majority of prose examples are in *The
Four Branches of the Mabinogi,* from roughly a century earlier.

No doubt Annwfn has been commonly understood as the
otherworld throughout most of Welsh history. But to underline
how rarely it's used in the surviving poetry, consider that we
have more of Cynddelw's work preserved in manuscript than

---

238 KUN-vayrth.

239 Go-GUN-vayrth.

240 Ich-EL-wir.

any of the other 27 *Gogynfeirdd* whose work has been edited. Not only is he the only bard to even mention Annwfn, but in all 3852 lines of his poetry that have survived, we only have one direct reference to the magical realm and a handful of indirect ones. Once again, that it was part of the older mythology and didn't accord with the Christian scheme appears to be the most likely reason for this scarcity.

Yet Cynddelw Brydydd Mawr, a proud and public Christian of his time, a famous bard who composed substantial poems in praise of God and saints alike, suggests he has access to some inner deep throughout the different periods of his bardic career. Of course, only a fraction of the poetry of the *Cynfeirdd* and *Gogynfeirdd* survive, so it's likely there were other examples of Annwfn, explicit and otherwise, that haven't come down to us. It at least appears to have been a traditional concept, firmly integrated into the beliefs of some of the most important court bards of the age.

Cynddelw began his career serving at the court of Madog ap Maredudd, king of Powys, during the 1150s, the last decade of Madog's reign.[241] If the scant evidence that survives is to be believed, he won the status of *pencerdd*, 'chief of bardic craft' at Madog's court in a competition against another bard who called him Cynddelw Brydydd 'Mawr', *mawr* meaning 'big'

---

241 Interestingly enough it was Madog's son, Cadwallon, who founded Abaty Cwm Hir in 1176, where *The Book of Taliesin* was created around a century and a half later.

here as opposed to 'great'. Cynddelw was a large man, and he earned his bardic epithet because of his great size, even though later generations came to use it to signify his greatness as a poet. Cynddelw literally means something like 'archetype', 'model' or 'example', and *prydydd* means 'trained bard' or 'poet of highest rank'. His name can therefore be understood to mean 'Archetype, the Great Poet', a name that lends itself to the mythical nature of the tradition he so powerfully embodied.

On attaining the status of *pencerdd*, Cynddelw would not only have taken on apprentices (a fact he was immensely proud of, according to some of his poems), but as was expected of bards since the days of Taliesin, he would have taken on the role of a chief celebrant of the king. In what may have been his first official poem of praise for Madog before the court, Cynddelw begins by proclaiming:

> I praise the lord with nine parts of my art,
>
> With nine awen, with nine kinds of song.[242]

There's no other mention of what these mystical subdivisions of art and awen are, although in a poem from around the same period, 'Preideu Annwn' (discussed later in this chapter) we find a description of the cauldron of the Head of Annwfn

---

242 My translation of the text in N.A. Jones & A.P. Owen (eds.), *Gwaith Cynddelw Brydydd Mawr I* (UWP 1991), 5.

that's heated by the breath of nine maidens. This could be what Cynddelw means by the nine parts of awen, especially considering its connection to air or breath. More commonly in the Celtic tradition, nine is one of those special numbers that appears to represent the natural divisions of a cosmic whole.[243] In the next line, Cynddelw sets about mythologising his patron:

> [I] praise a brave man of Gogrfan's courage . . .

Gogrfan is one of Madog's great ancestors, and Cynddelw conflates this ancient figure with Madog himself, transforming him in the audience's imagination from a mere mortal into the embodiment of an ancient and powerful lineage. So far, this is all standard stuff for a praise poem. But at the end of this first section, Cynddelw gives some rare insight into what he believes he can accomplish through such finely wrought poetry:

> Madog is a pilgrim in the protection
> and metal-work of my song,
>
> The honour-song of his praise is made fair
> so that it will never be forgotten.

In the first line, Cynddelw talks about the *'metal-work of my song'*, depicting the bards as craftsmen, specialists in a physical craft that had tangible effects, one of which was to make Madog a *'pilgrim in . . . my song'*, implying the king undertakes a sacred

---

243   See Alwyn & Brinley Rees, *Celtic Heritage* (Thames and Hudson 1991), 192-6.

journey *within* Cynddelw's protective poetry. If Cynddelw is being more literal than metaphorical, with his poetic craft he can summon a sacred space within which Madog is a pilgrim, journeying for the sake of his soul's purity. Through their poetry, bards such as Cynddelw often sought to construct the mythological architecture of the court, granting their patrons access to that imagined space inhabited by great heroes and mystic druids. Cynddelw implicitly understood the power of publicly mythologising a nobleman, not only the psychological impact on the man himself but also the way he was seen by his subjects.

That bards could conjure such a depth in their poetry is implied elsewhere in Cynddelw's work. Regardless of his efforts to protect Madog, the king's fate did not differ from other mortals. In 1160, Madog died, tipping the kingdom of Powys into an instability that soon toppled over into a terminal decline with the sudden death of Madog's son and heir, Llywelyn. It's not clear how Llywelyn met his end, but with no successor to hold power, the once substantial kingdom of Powys broke apart as Madog's remaining sons and nephews took possession of its different territories. This would have been a devastating moment for Cynddelw, to see the court and kingdom he had served disappear before his very eyes.

Soon after, Cynddelw attempted to bring the main families of the kingdom to some accord. In the poem 'The

Lineages of Powys', Cynddelw praises those noble families who would have been trying to cling to some hope of unity in such uncertain times. He lends them his full support as a chief of the bardic craft:

> I present to you a poem of praise.
>
> Your gifts support me,
>
> You who serve a gift to soldiers:
>
> May God's blessing be with you, princes!
>
> It is customary for a bard to bless men of noble descent.
>
> I present to you a poem of praise,
> men of Powys who charge in battle,
>
> Eager and severe men of Argoed:
>
> My greatness, my fame, demands it,
>
> My griefs, my passions rouse me.[244]

He lists each of the fourteen families, recalling ancient battles fought by glorious ancestors, emphasising how they, as their living descendants, are worthy of the same honour and praise, telling them of their common heritage in the golden age court bards such as he preserved in memory. Towards the end of his list of families, he declaims:

---

244 My translation of the text in Owen & Parry (1991), 119.

The eleventh fruit of my awen,
the eleventh fruit of my passion

That provide for the role given to me:

The sum of my song, of my craft,
of my ability as a poet is given

For the one beautiful as a hawk,
for the retinue of Gwalch's family.

The twelfth superior ones who circle the splendid,
fair one of the palisade.

Fighting fiercely in the face of a bloody wound:

Strong their claim because of the man
who no longer lives,

Descendants of Gwriaeth Ysgoyw,
with their dented shields.[245]

The very poem itself was proof of the continuity of the old order. In his ritual declamation, Cynddelw elevates these families to the realm of ideals, leading them from the hard and mundane world and lighting their way to the mythical land of honour and dignity. His task was to create a sacred space in the imagination where those present were still worthy of dignity and privilege. In the absence of a king or prince, it appears as if a court bard of Cynddelw's stature could become not only the focal point of public unity, but a guide to the otherworld of their noble ideals.

---

245   Ibid. 123.

Yet for all of Cynddelw's conjuring in the face of tragedy, there was still no king in a court for him to serve, and soon after the death of Madog and his son, Cynddelw moved on to a patron worthy of his craft. He was still in his prime as a poet, and his renown ensured him a position at the court of Owain, king of Gwynedd, grandfather of Llywelyn the Great. For the following decade, Cynddelw served Owain faithfully, in one of his praise poems evoking the same sacred space he had conjured for the Powys nobility:

> A mirror of authority, the one raised on mead,
> born fortunate.
>
> A mirror of courtesy, swift hawk,
>
> A mirror of the deep awen of deep memories,
>
> A great mirror, swift soldier, . . .[246]

The third line conveys a complex of ideas in a very few words. The Welsh original reads '*Yn ail awen ddofn o ddwfn gofiain*', *dofn* and *dwfn* respectively being the feminine and masculine forms of *dwfn*, and although used as an adjective here, it's the same word used as a noun in the second part of Annwfn. Initially, this *dwfn* can be read as meaning 'profound', but with the further implication of 'deep', that is the 'inner deep' of Annwfn. These 'deep memories', being old, profound

---

246   Ibid. II, 8.

and somehow of the otherworld, carry a similar meaning to that implied in 'The Lineages of Powys', where the past is an idyllic realm, a golden age brimming with ancestral power. 'Awen ddofn' further amplifies the connection to Annwfn, the inspiration taken from these memories also being of the deep, of Annwfn.

It appears to have been Cynddelw's destiny to serve as a court bard in all three mediaevel Welsh kingdoms. When Owain Gwynedd died in 1170, exactly a decade after the death of Madog ap Maredudd, Cynddelw would have been a man in his full maturity, still in possession of the greatest bardic skill of his age. No patron could be worthy of such a regal bard other than a king, and it was natural therefore that he spent the last chapter in his long and storied career with the Lord Rhys, prince of Deheubarth,[247] the kingdom that made up most of South Wales. Lord Rhys ap Gruffydd was one of the most important princes of the period and, after the death of Owain Gwynedd, the most powerful man in Wales, the king of the southern lands in all but name.

In 1176, during Cynddelw's time at the court of Lord Rhys, the earliest recorded eisteddfod[248] was held. To this day, the eisteddfodau are the main cultural festivals of Wales, and can range from small, local events, to national and international

---

247   De-HAY-barth.

248   Ay-STETH-vod.

competitions in literature, music and the arts. There would
have been similar competitions held throughout Welsh history,
but the earliest account we have is of the Lord Rhys' eisteddfod.
Here's what the thirteenth-century *Brut y Tywysogion* ('History
of the Princes') tells us:

> At Christmas in that year, Lord Rhys ap Gruffydd held
> an excellent court in Aberteifi,[249] in the castle, and set up
> two kinds of contests there: one between poets and bards,
> another between harpers and musicians and pipers and
> all manner of other types of musical art, and he gave
> two chairs to the winners and he honoured them with
> abundant gifts.[250]

As the resident *pencerdd* and licensed master to a troop of
apprentices, it probably would have fallen to a bard such
as Cynddelw to judge the poetry competitions. That such a
significant cultural event took place, one that drew participants
from as far afield as Ireland and France, shows how much energy
and vigour there was in the traditional Welsh arts. At this
event, Cynddelw would doubtlessly have been acknowledged as
the grand master of his age.

It's during this period, in a poem in praise of the Lord
Rhys, that we find the only explicit reference to Annwfn to
have survived in Cynddelw's work. Rhys was lord over Dyfed,

---

249   Abair-TAY-vi. Called Cardigan in English.

250   My translation of the text in Thomas Jones (ed.), *Brut y Tywysogion: Red Book of Herg-est Version* (UWP 1973).

the territory that's very close to Annwfn in *The First Branch of the Mabinogi*. This one explicit reference to Annwfn may be an acknowledgement of that local tradition: Aberteifi was literally a stone's throw away from Glyn Cuch,[251] the valley where Pwyll meets the king of Annwfn. In his poem, Cynddelw describes the role of the inner deep:

> Powerfully does my song go forth in completeness
>
> To praise fully the king that deserves it.
>
> In renowned praise full of dignity,
>
> With ready awen in an ode of fair, pure poetry;
>
> In Annwfn, in the deep, in the depth, it judges.
>
> Other bards do not impoverish it,
>
> It is this bard that declaims it.[252]

According to Cynddelw, the inner deep of the world is the place where divine awen lives. Not only that, but awen judges in Annwfn. It gives the bard the necessary insight to judge the patron's worthiness of praise. The awen will not be roused if the patron's not a fitting object of the bard's refined adulation. We are very much in the realm of *The First Branch* here, where Annwfn is a place of high and noble ideals, certainly not in the realm of

---

251   Glin Keech.

252   My translation of the text edited in Jones & Owen (1995), 167.

How Culhwch Won Olwen, where it's akin to hell. The deep awen is of the same nature as the inner deep from whence it comes, and the inspiration it confers, perhaps unsurprisingly, is that of perfection, beauty, honour and dignity. It gives a perspective on the ideal and the true, on all the best in human life.

It's difficult to say how widespread this understanding of awen and Annwfn was, not only in Cynddelw's time but throughout the long history of the Welsh bardic tradition. Most sources simply refer to a depth, and even though this is very suggestive, there seems to have been a general reluctance to mention Annwfn specifically by name.

Beyond Cynddelw's work, there is only one other poem that explicitly names Annwfn as the source of the bardic awen, and that is 'The Hostile Confederacy' in *The Book of Taliesin,* a poem that could well have been reworked by Llywarch ap Llywelyn. Llywarch almost certainly knew Cynddelw, and may even have been apprenticed to him for a time. As Cynddelw was coming to the end of his career, Llywarch's was just beginning, and the older poet would have been at least an influence on the younger. Cynddelw was the greatest bard of the age, and Llywarch was the only one to even come close to matching his stature.

That almost all our references in poetry to the inner deep is in work by or connected to either Cynddelw or Llywarch is very telling. It suggests they may have formed an important link in an old lineage that had some connection to the Taliesin myth and its related concepts of Annwfn and awen. In 'The Hostile Confederacy' the legendary Taliesin tells us it was God who determined this relationship between Annwfn and awen, setting out all of the divisions of inspiration in the inner deep:

> In Annwfn He set them out,
>
> In Annwfn He made them,
>
> In Annwfn below the earth,
>
> In the air above the earth.[253]

In the more open-minded parts of mediaevel Christian culture, it appears to have been accepted that if Annwfn is the otherworldly source of the divine awen, then God must have made it so. Again, this isn't the demonic Annwfn of *How Culhwch Won Olwen*, but the idyllic Annwfn of *The First Branch*. Just as Pwyll simply follows Arawn into the inner deep in that story, we can assume these poets likewise considered it close by, imminent and accessible from anywhere.

For Cynddelw, this world-within-the-world is a place of memory and deep inspiration, a depth he can reach into and draw out the full meaning of his king, sensing the form of an ideal hero in the mortal man. As suggested elsewhere by

---

253 My translation of the text in Haycock (2015), 114.

the legendary Taliesin in 'The Hostile Confederacy', this is not only done in the moment of a poem's creation but also in the moment if its performance:

> I sing awen,
>
> I bring it out of the deep.[254]

As Cynddelw mentions in one of his court poems, this ability resulted from being *'steeped in the mystic ways of Ceridwen's crafts'*.[255] The whole mystical understanding of how bards drew on the awen of Annwfn was bound up with Ceridwen's myth. Although it was impossible for him to adopt the title, Cynddelw can be understood as a type of priest with access not only to a divine power but also an inner deep of cultural memory, a sacred space of traditional ideals with which he can bless his patrons.

As we've already seen, by the twelfth century, some court bards were performing poetry in the guise of the legendary Taliesin, boasting of his learning and enlightenment, and of his otherworldly nature. One of these legendary poems in *The*

---

254   Ibid. 119.

255   My translation of the text in Jones & Owen (1995), 290-316.

Book of Taliesin is 'Preideu Annwfyn' ('The Spoils of Annwfn'), a long and obscure text full of riddles, allusions, and ambiguous references to things we simply don't understand. But for all of its esoteric quality, we can make some sense of parts of it. The legendary Taliesin appears to be recounting one of his adventures to the otherworld: a mission with King Arthur to steal a magic cauldron. The first section introduces the basic narrative:

> I praise the Lord, Ruler of the kingdom,
>
> Who has spread His dominion over the whole world.
>
> Well-kept was Gwair's prison in Caer Siddi
>
> Throughout the story of Pwyll and Pryderi.
>
> Before him, no one had gone there —
>
> Into the heavy, grey chain guarding the best of youths.
>
> And he was singing sadly before the spoils of Annwfn,
>
> And our poetic prayer shall continue until Doom.
>
> Three full ship-loads of Prydwen we went into it:
>
> But for seven, none came back from Caer Siddi.[256]

The poem goes on for another fifty lines in much the same fashion, and anyone hearing it for the first time would likely be at a total loss. It's as if the poet wants to baffle the

---

256   My translation of the text in Haycock (2015), 435.

audience, challenging them to pay attention and keep up. After the standard opening in praise of God, we are led straight into ambiguity:

> Well-kept was Gwair's prison in Caer Siddi
>
> Throughout the story of Pwyll and Pryderi.

The name for this otherworldly prison, Caer Siddi,[257] literally means 'Fairy-mound Fortress': *siddi* is borrowed from the Irish *sidh*, the name for ancient burial mounds that in Irish myth are entrances to the otherworld.[258] We can safely assume that Caer Siddi is at least in Annwfn because it's mentioned in another of the legendary poems, 'Golychaf-i Gulwydd', 'I Petition God', where the legendary Taliesin tells us:

> My song in Caer Siddi is harmonious;
>
> Sickness and old age do not harm those who are there, . . .[259]

This is clearly the timeless otherworld and land of the ever-youthful. To return to 'The Spoils of Annwfn', we don't know exactly who Gwair was, but he is mentioned in one of the bardic triads:

---

257 Ka-ir SITH-i.

258 See Sims-Williams (2011), 66-78.

259 My translation of the text in Haycock (2015), 277.

The Three Supreme Prisoners of the Island of Britain:
Llŷr Half-Speech, who was imprisoned by Euroswydd,
and the second, Mabon son of Modron,
and the third Gwair son of Gweirioedd.[260]

Just like many other characters mentioned in the mediaevel catalogue of triads, Gwair's tale is now lost to us, but as someone imprisoned in Caer Siddi, he bears some resemblance to other figures in Welsh myth. In the *Third Branch of the Mabinogi*, Pryderi, named alongside Gwair in the poem, is also imprisoned in an enchanted fortress. Or, as the triad itself tells us, Mabon, who was imprisoned in a fortress on the banks of the River Severn. Only the oldest and wisest of animals, the Salmon of Llyn Lliw, knew the location of his prison, suggesting its peculiar nature.

In conflating the stories of Gwair and Pryderi at least, some scholars concluded the poem was a confused rendition of an original story where Gwair and Pryderi are names for the same character.[261] Another reason could be that this anonymous bard is alluding to different versions of the same basic tale where a noble youth is captive in an enchanted prison, perhaps assuming those learned enough in bardic lore would also see the connection. This would suggest that, much like modern

---

260   Rachel Bromwich, *Trioedd Ynys Prydein* (UWP 2006).

261   See W.J. Gruffydd, *Rhiannon* (UWP 1952), 13, 18, and in general the chapter on Rhiannon.

scholars, bards and storytellers of the past appreciated how the same narrative patterns appeared in different poems and tales.

The next few lines tell us a little more about this mysterious prisoner, Gwair:

> Before him, no one had gone there —
>
> into the heavy, grey chain guarding the best of youths.
>
> And he was singing sadly before the spoils of Annwfn,
>
> And our poetic prayer shall continue until Doom.

It's the ambiguous third line that gives the poem its title, 'The Spoils of Annwfn'. The Welsh word for 'spoils', *preiddeu* could also mean 'herds', literally herds of cattle. The reason it's hard to confine it to one meaning is that the poem mentions at least one treasure from the otherworld, that being a magic cauldron, and at least one herd animal, that being a mythical ox. In later folklore, the Welsh otherworld is often described as an idyllic place full of riches, but also a place where fairy cattle live.[262] Of course, the line could refer to both things; a typical bardic play on words.

The fourth line describes how the sacred poetry of the bardic tradition shall continue until the end of time, and this appears to be connected to the captive youth. Gwair sings sadly

---

262   See the story of Llyn Barfog in John Rhys, *Celtic Folklore* Vol. 1 (1901), 141-6.

over the great treasures of Annwfn, his longing being to share these wonders or for his life before captivity; perhaps both. Gwair's mournful song could be the *'poetic prayer'* that *'shall continue until Doom'*. The youth's sadness is in part caused by his separation from this world, the main rift being that in time, and his song is a symbol for how awen arises from the grief of separation between the mortal and immortal realms. Perhaps for this poet at least, the yearning for communion between the two is awen, the latent force that inspires the bard.

The last couplet in this section alludes to the story behind this ambiguous poem, which appears to be an incursion into the otherworld:

> Three full ship-loads of Prydwen we went into it:
>
> But for seven, none came back from Caer Siddi.

Prydwen is King Arthur's ship, and here three full shiploads of Arthur's men went with their king and Taliesin into the otherworld, where there was such a fierce battle that only seven returned. There appears to have been a few reasons for this raid on Annwfn, perhaps the most obvious being that Arthur was seeking the rescue of Gwair, just as he sought to rescue Mabon in *How Culhwch Won Olwen*. Considering how Gwair's song could represent the grief-laden yearning of awen, the mission to rescue Gwair from Annwfn could likewise be a metaphor for the challenges a bard faces as he seeks the treasured awen. It's not clear if the metaphor can be extended this far, particularly as it's drawn from such an ambiguous poem, but it at least illustrates the relationship between bard, awen and Annwfn.

Another reason for Arthur and Taliesin's incursion appears to have been their attempt to steal the otherworld's treasures. The story of a Welsh king crossing the sea to fight a battle with a foe who possesses a magic cauldron is actually very similar to other mediaevel stories, such as *The Second Branch of the Mabinogi*,[263] one of the shorter episodes in *How Culhwch Won Olwen*,[264] and more broadly several Irish tales.[265] In *The Second Branch* in particular, Taliesin is even one of the minor characters in the story. Bendigeidfran crosses to Ireland to rescue his sister Branwen from her abusive marriage to King Matholwch. In a great battle where the Irish use a cauldron of rebirth to bring their dead warriors back to life, the Welsh nonetheless prevail, but it is a hollow victory. The whole of Ireland has been devastated and Bendigeidfran has been mortally wounded. He orders the remaining seven companions, Taliesin amongst them, to cut off his head and return to Wales,

---

263   Davies (2007), 25-34.

264   Ibid. 208-9.

265   See Patrick Sims-Williams, 'The Early Welsh Arthurian Poems', in Rachel Bromwich et al (eds.), *The Arthur of the Welsh* (UWP 1991), 55-7; also Proinsias Mac Cana, *Branwen Daughter of Llŷr* (UWP 1958), 45-6.

where they will be magically feasted for 87 years before they bury his head in London.

When we compare these events with 'The Spoils of Annwfn' we find both share the same basic story:

1. A king of Britain

2. goes on a voyage with Taliesin and a host of men

3. to fight a foe who has a magic cauldron.

4. The resulting carnage is so terrible

5. only seven return, Taliesin amongst them.

Like other basic narratives that are found in different texts, we could read an older myth here. It may not be explicit in all the versions we've looked at so far, but the voyage is either figuratively or literally to Annwfn. Ireland, and islands generally were otherworldly places,[266] and at least took the place of Annwfn in successive versions of the story. Again, this suggests that Annwfn wasn't thought of as a distant otherworld or underworld, but a dimension that's always imminent, regardless of location.

In the next section of the poem, Taliesin appears to have gained entry to Caer Siddi:

---

266   See Sims-Williams (2011), 63-6.

> I'm splendid of fame — my song was heard
>
> In the four-cornered fort revolving to face the four directions.[267]

As a four-cornered fort that revolves to face the four directions, there appears to be some type of alignment taking place in Annwfn, perhaps even an astronomical one if the directions are here sighted by the stars. We have already seen how the name Caer Siddi implies the idea of a Neolithic monument, and many such monuments were built in alignment with astronomical events, such as the Winter Solstice at Sí an Bhrú[268] in Ireland or the Summer Solstice at Bryn Celli Ddu[269] in Wales. A turning otherworld fortress also suggests the night-sky itself, the great wheel of stars rolling around the horizon. Either way, here in performance, the legendary Taliesin conjures a cosmically aligned space within which he gives voice to his poem, and where he evokes one of the great treasures of Annwfn:

> My first declamation was about the cauldron
>
> That's kindled by the breath of nine maidens.[270]

The natural assumption would be that the 'breath of nine maidens' was a metaphor for awen, if not a nod to the nine

---

267 My translation of the text in Haycock (2015), 435.

268 Shee an Vrew. Called New Grange in English.

269 Brin KELL-i Thee.

270 My translation of the text in Haycock (2015), 435.

muses of Greek tradition, but if this is the bardic cauldron we would expect awen to come out of it, not be required to make it boil.[271] Unless, of course, this is describing a different phase in the process of bardic service, where awen has already been achieved, and now put to magical use. Taliesin tells us a little more about this cauldron:

> The cauldron of the Head of Annwn, what is its nature,
>
> Dark edged and set with pearls?
>
> It won't boil a coward's food, that is not its destiny:
>
> Into it was thrust Lleog's flashing sword,
>
> And it was left behind in Lleminog's hand.
>
> And before hell's gate, lamps burned.
>
> And when we went with Arthur, famed in adversity,
>
> But for seven, none came back from the Mead-Feast Fort.[272]

Here the entrance to Annwfn is called the Mead-Feast Fort, a place where bards would be eternally feasted, suggesting the indigenous concept of Annwfn. But it's also called 'hell's gate', probably both in anticipation of the coming carnage and also

---

271   In another typically obscure passage in the poem 'Angar Kyfundawt', the legendary bard tells us about the enchanted cauldrons of Gwion and Afagddu: 'Their cauldrons they make / That boil without fire. / They make their materials / for ever and ever'. My translation of the text in Haycock (2015), 110-11.

272   Ibid. 436.

echoing the Christian view of the otherworld. In this poem at least, Annwfn is being portrayed both as the native otherworld and also the place of devils and danger.

As already mentioned, there is a brief episode in *How Culhwch Won Olwen* that bears some resemblance to the basic story here. One of Arthur's tasks in the story is to retrieve a special cauldron from Ireland. He sets off with a small force in his ship Prydwen and after landing they make for the house of Diwrnach,[273] the cauldron's keeper. When Diwrnach refuses to hand over the cauldron, one of Arthur's men, Llenlleog,[274] grabs Arthur's special sword — called Caledfwlch[275] in the Welsh tradition — and swings it around, killing Diwrnach and all his retinue. The hosts of Ireland come to fight them and when Arthur is victorious, they all flee, leaving the Welsh warriors to return with the cauldron full of Irish treasure.

Both 'The Spoils of Annwfn' and this episode mention sword-wielding characters bearing similar names. In *How Culhwch Won Olwen*, the swordsman is Lleminog, yet in the poem there are two characters who appear to share very similar names, Lleog[276] and Llenlleog.[277] These could all be variations

---

273 DEEWR-nach.

274 Llen-LLAY-og.

275 Kal-ED-vwlch.

276 LLAY-og.

277 Llen-LLAY-og.

on the same basic character who wields the magic sword in the battle for the magic cauldron.

There are a few other sources that confirm there was once a common narrative that these various texts have grown out of, the most important being the mediaevel list known as 'The Thirteen Treasures of Britain',[278] where the seventh treasure is described as:

> The Cauldron of Dyrnwch the Giant: if meat for a coward were put in it to boil, it would never boil; but if meat for a brave man were put in it, it would boil quickly (and thus the brave could be distinguished from the cowardly).[279]

This cauldron is almost identical to the one in 'The Spoils of Annwfn', and its keeper, Dyrnwch,[280] bears a very similar name to that of the Irish cauldron-keeper, Diwrnach, in *How Culhwch Won Olwen*. If we add this additional episode to the basic narrative, we can reconstruct a far more detailed account of the myth that sits behind 'The Spoils of Annwfn':

1. A king of Britain

2. voyages to the otherworld

---

278   The other two references are 1) the character Wrnach the Giant from another episode in *How Culhwch Won Olwen*, Davies (2015), 200-2; 2) the character Afarnach from one of the earliest Arthurian poems known as 'Pa Gur?', N.A. Jones (ed.), *Arthur in Early Welsh Poetry* (MHRA 2019), 29-59.

279   'The Thirteen Treasures of the Island of Britain' in Bromwich (2006), 259.

280   DERN-wch.

3. with his bard and a host of men

4. to fight a giant

5. and steal his magic cauldron.

6. In the attack, a champion thrusts a special sword into the cauldron

7. and / or uses it to kill the giant.

8. The resulting carnage is so terrible

9. only seven return, the bard amongst them.[281]

This simple story gives some possible insight into who this mysterious Head of Annwfn was and what became of him. As a giant he is already supernatural in nature, and like Bendigeidfran in *The Second Branch* has access to the time-out-of-time. As Head of Annwfn and keeper of the magic cauldron, he would also have been the keeper of awen, here described as nourishment for the brave. Once again, this cauldron and its awen can be read as a symbol for the Welsh bardic tradition.

The main function of these ancient poets was to celebrate the bravery of their patrons, and here this praise is a type of symbolic nourishment provided for the warrior elite who thrived on honour and fame. This particular cauldron isn't feeding the bard with awen, but the bard is using awen to

---

281 This reconstruction doesn't account for all the different variations, and other choices could be made as to how other elements are incorporated.

heat up a feast for his patrons. It is perhaps natural for such a vessel to not only give nourishment in the form of the awen-inspired praise, but to require a mythic heroism to obtain it, as described in the next section of the poem:

> I scorn the pathetic men involved in religious literature,
>
> Those who had no knowledge of Arthur's great feat at the Glass Fort:
>
> Six thousand men standing on the fortress wall;
>
> It was hard to speak with their watchman.
>
> Three full ship-loads of Prydwen went with Arthur:
>
> But for seven, none returned from the Fort of Restriction.[282]

This section begins with a dig at the monks of mediaeval Wales and their ignorance of Arthur's heroic attack on the otherworld. As a name for Annwfn, the Glass Fort recalls Revelation 21:18: 'and the [heavenly] city was pure gold, like unto clear glass', pouring further scorn on those daft monks who don't even know a reference to the Bible when they hear one. Beyond scripture, there is a much more obvious precursor to this episode in the *Historia Brittonum* (828 CE), where we are told of the colonising of Ireland:

---

282 My translation of the text in Haycock (2015), 436.

After [the Tuatha Dé Dannan] came three sons of a
Spanish soldier with thirty ships, each of which contained
thirty wives; and having remained there during the space
of a year, there appeared to them, in the middle of the sea,
a tower of glass, the summit of which seemed covered
with men, to whom they often spoke, but received no
answer. At length they determined to besiege the tower;
and after a year's preparation, advanced towards it,
with the whole number of their ships, and all the women,
one ship only excepted, which had been wrecked, and in
which were thirty men, and as many women; but when
all had disembarked on the shore which surrounded the
tower, the sea opened and swallowed them up. Ireland,
however, was peopled, to the present period, from the
family remaining in the vessel which was wrecked.[283]

This anonymous poet appears to be accomplishing two things
here, not only blending Celtic myth with imagery drawn from
the Christian tradition, but also testing the church men with
their book learning to see if they realise what he's doing.
Throughout the following sections of the poem, Taliesin
returns to his criticism of Christian scholarship, as he does
in several other legendary poems. The balance between both
mythologies appears to be finely struck in this poem; not only is
it a full evocation of the pagan otherworld, but it's described on
occasion in terms drawn directly from the Christian tradition.
This may not be intentional on the poet's part because such

---

283   Anon., *Historia Brittonum*, trans. in *Six Old English Chronicles*, ed. J. A. Giles. (London,
1848).

imagery would have been common-place, simply part of the cultural furniture of mediaevel Wales. On the other hand, it may have staved off the worst accusations of heresy from the more reactionary Christians of the age.

'The Spoils of Annwfn' sits in the middle of a tangled web of myth and tradition, probably only fully comprehensible to those few who had a bardic education. We can assume that only some of the references piled up in this long poem would have been understood by a broader audience, leading them to the obvious conclusion that they were not amongst the chosen few initiated into the bardic mysteries. Of course, for those steeped in the myths of the bardic tradition it is a work rich in implied knowledge and allusions to symbolic meaning. In this sense, it's quite an elitist poem, separating those in the know from those that are definitely not. The message to that broader audience would have been that they had just been given a tantalising glimpse of the bard's secret knowledge, and no more.

Ceridwen isn't mentioned at all in 'The Spoils of Annwfn', and like 'The Battle of the Trees' this suggests we have a poem from a different lineage in Taliesin's myth. Where one branch of the oral tradition, perhaps the most common, developed the story of Ceridwen, this perhaps less common lineage drew on the myth of a magic cauldron taken during a raid on the otherworld. Branches of this lineage may well have overlapped with Ceridwen's myth at times, but others may also have remained separate. We can at least trace some elements of 'The Spoils of Annwfn' into poems by later bards.

We find the main flourishing of the mediaevel myth of Taliesin in the legendary poems of *The Book of Taliesin*. Most of these poems, if not all of them, were probably written down sometime around the late twelfth century, with the final manuscript itself copied early in the fourteenth. From then on, we find a range of Taliesin poetry in later manuscripts, most of it exploring and developing the same themes that we find in *The Book of Taliesin*.

Sometime around the 1400s, an unknown poet composed a poem called 'Cadair Aur Taliesin',[284] 'Taliesin's Golden Chair'.[285] Just like the legendary poems, it's composed in Taliesin's voice, once again suggesting that anyone performing it would have adopted the dramatic persona of the great bard:

> My speech is perfect, truthful language,
>
> My clothes are purple from the land of Paradise,
> from the flowers of trees.
>
> I have a golden chair in Caer Sidydd,

---

284 KAD-ire eye-r . . .

285 See the discussion on '*cadair*' in Chapter 8.

In a blessed circle, turning between
three elements / in three similar [circles]. [286]

The third line here is clearly echoing the name for the otherworldly fortress in 'The Spoils of Annwfn', but instead of *Caer Siddi*, in this later poem we have *Caer Sidydd*,[287] which doesn't mean 'Fairy-mound Fortress', but 'The Astrologers Fortress', as intriguing a name as the original. Yet, even though there has been a change, there also appears to be a continuity in meaning. As discussed earlier, the *siddi* in the earlier version is derived from the Irish *sidh*, the name given to ancient burial mounds often built in alignment with astronomical events. The latter name, *Caer Sidydd*, 'The Astrologers Fortress', suggests these later bards still understood this otherworldly fortress to have astronomical connections, regardless of the change in name. There is also a continuity in style from *The Book of Taliesin* to these later poems, as we see in this first section of the poem, which is as ambiguous as anything we find in the preceding centuries.

The last line contains two possible meanings. The original Welsh reads '*Mewn gwenrod yn troi rhwng tri elfydd*' and the problematic word here is *elfydd*. A standard meaning is 'world' or 'land', but it can also mean 'element' or 'that which cannot

---

286   My translation of the text in Gruffydd(1997),158.

287   Ka-ir SID-ith.

be resolved into simpler parts'.[288] But as the original editor of the poem, G.F. Gruffydd, points out, *elfydd* can also mean 'similar' or 'alike',[289] which would suggest that the otherworldly space being evoked here is a nested set of four circles.

Yet again, if the meaning is 'element', this isn't a reference to the four Aristotelian elements of earth, air, fire and water, but three elements that appear to turn in a circle around the bard. This basic scheme draws on the very ancient symbol of the bisected circle and its centre. Consider the Christian Celtic cross or the Hindu or Celtic swastika as examples: each comprises several arms connected by a central axis, suggesting rotation around a still centre. In a very simple sense, we can read these types of symbols as attempts to unify the contrasting states of movement and stillness.

We find the same tension implied in the imagery of 'Taliesin's Golden Chair': the great bard's seat is the still centre around which the elements or fundamental cosmic powers turn, again implying Taliesin is the personification of a universal principle that's at the heart of creation. The image at least draws on basic themes found in religious symbols and amplifies the mystical connotations of the poem.

Even though we hear echoes of *The Book of Taliesin*, it's hard to say how widespread such ideas were during the

---

288   *University of Wales Dictionary.*

289   Gruffydd (1997), 581.

mediaeval period; whether they originated in the legendary poems or were part of a broader tradition; whether these later poems were mere obscurities or central to the common Taliesin myth. We find several variations and re-workings of similar passages in several manuscripts, suggesting there was at the very least a vibrant subculture that made up the more mystical strand in the Taliesin tradition, almost certainly adapting inherited pieces of oral poetry. The influence of *The Book of Taliesin* can still be seen in the late fifteenth century, where we see a further development in the *Caer Siddi* / *Caer Sidydd* idea.

This following stanza is taken from an elegy for a poet by Dafydd Epynt, composed around 1480:

He casts aside his spear [and the] four elements,

He tends the silk of Cadair Sidydd.

A name was upon his lips for the voice of Taliesin

In a blessed way for our awenydd.[290]

Cadair Sidydd, 'The Astrologer's Chair' is a further evolution of the original term *Caer Siddi,* 'The Fairy-mound Fortress', having passed through the intervening form *Caer Sidydd,* 'The Astrologer's Fortress'. Once again, it appears as if a basic meaning has been preserved in these names, that being the

---

290   My translation of the text in Owen Thomas, *Gwaith Dafydd Epynt* (Prifysgol Cymru 2023), 36.

connection between an otherworldly place and astronomical alignments that either revolve around or are at least observed from the otherworld. According to Dafydd Epynt, the dead poet's soul now lives in Annwfn, *Cadair Sidydd* perhaps being a more acceptable name that avoided connotations of a Christian hell.

When we consider the other descriptions of Annwfn in mediaeval Welsh literature, there are some suggestions that it was a type of 'land of the dead', perhaps Lleu's transmigration into an eagle in *The Fourth Branch of the Mabinogi* being the most obvious. Yet in *The First Branch* there is no sense that Pwyll is entering the land of souls. Perhaps the confusion arises out of our modern understanding of terms such as life, death and soul; these may not agree with how the Brythonic culture of the past thought of such things.

Dafydd Epynt describes how in death the poet *'casts aside his spear [and the] four elements'*, that is he relinquishes his material form that was, according to the classical learning spread by Christianity, made up of the four elements. The earliest mention of the elements is in the work of Empedocles, a fifth-century BCE Greek philosopher who described them as the divine materials of existence. Aristotle then developed this basic scheme by adding the fifth element of ether. The concept was later adopted by Islamic scholars of the late first millennium who transformed it into a type of magical process.

This in turn feeds back into the European tradition where it maintains its magical overtones, ultimately becoming a part of Renaissance mysticism and alchemy. We certainly find knowledge of the classical elements in Wales as early as the twelfth century. For example, Llywarch ap Llywelyn mentions them in one of his formal praise poems:

> Christ, son of Mary, caused me to be made
> from my four materials,
>
> deep and powerful awen.[291]

These are the fundamental elements of creation as described in Church learning, and therefore the basic materials of the human body as far as the mediaevel world was concerned. Through Jesus's all-powerful awen the poet was created from these four elements, that is awen in its most fundamental condition as the very force of divine creation. In the legendary poems we also find the four elements making up Taliesin's body, this time in a poem that doesn't appear to be connected to Llywarch ap Llywelyn. Taliesin states that God created his *'. . . seven substances of fire and earth and water and air / And mist and flowers in the prosperous wind.'*[292] The common idea in all of these poems is that the four elements are the foundations of physical existence, and therefore don't belong in Annwfn.

---

291 My translation of the text in Jones & Jones (1991), 220.

292 My translation of the text in Haycock (2015), 516.

In Llywarch ap Llywelyn's case, they accompany birth into material creation. Considering the image of the bard sitting at the centre of the three circulating elements in 'Taliesin's Golden Chair', he is the immaterial witness, the timeless centre within and from which the outer elements are experienced. Likewise,[293] if Gwion's animal transformations are symbols for the three domains of land, sea and sky, he sheds them at death before Ceridwen delivers him to his liminal, Annwfian state. And in Dafydd Epynt's thinking at least, the four elements are likewise cast off *before* entry to Caer Siddi.

In Elis Gruffydd's sixteenth-century *Cronicl*, he confirms much of what has been alluded to concerning this inner deep:

> *Some people hold the opinion and maintain firmly that Merlin was a spirit in human form, who was in that shape from the time of Vortigern until the beginning of King Arthur's time when he disappeared. After that, this spirit appeared again in the time of Maelgwn Gwynedd at which time he is called Taliesin, who is said to be alive yet in a place called Caer Sidia. Thence, he appeared a third time in the days of Merfyn Frych son of Esyllt, whose son he was said to be, and in this period he was called Merlin the Mad. From that day to this, he is said to be resting in Caer Sidia, whence certain people believe firmly that he will rise up once again before doomsday.*[294]

---

293   As discussed in Chapter 7. Transformation.

294   Quoted in Ford (1992), 4.

This reads like the story of a Welsh Dalai Lama, a reincarnating spiritual leader who returns several times to the mortal realm to teach and bring about spiritual harmony. If this is the place the great bard resides between incarnations, then it would follow that it's not a final destination at one's death, but a place the soul passes through on the way to further incarnations.

As Sioned Davis notes, in Breton culture, a cousin to that of the Welsh, when someone passed over it was said that they had 'gone to Annwn',[295] perhaps just to visit. According to some Welsh bards working in the Taliesin tradition, this required a casting off of the elements of material creation before access to the timeless and immaterial realm of Annwfn was possible. To reside in Caer Siddi was to pass beyond the realm of embodied existence and its entanglements in time. By implication, physical bodies are beings in time, while the non-physical are necessarily timeless.

The main difference between Annwfn and our own realm appears to be a temporal one. Whereas our plane of existence is characterised by ageing and death, 'sickness and old age' do not affect those in Caer Siddi. It appears to be the place of eternal renewal, where pristine life continues without the effects of time and its changes. By contrast, to partake of the mortal realm

---

295 Davies (2007), 229.

is to by swept up in the turbulent currents of transformation, to be spun in the cycles of birth and death and to know the suffering of experience. As a native of Annwfn, Taliesin is able to maintain the pristine vigour and consciousness of his homeland, even as he tumbles through the mortal realm with the dizzying velocity of all embodied beings. He does so with the assured joy of one who knows he will inevitably return to the blessed halls of Caer Siddi.

CHAPTER 10

Rebirth

... this was the spirit of Gwion Bach,
who had been in the belly of Ceridwen, ...

Gwion Bach's most transformative experience is that of death and rebirth. Nine months after Ceridwen eats him as a grain of wheat, she gives birth to a baby boy, and just like the infant Moses, he is set adrift on a river and carried out to sea. It's only when he's discovered on the shore and given the name Taliesin that he goes through his final transformation: reincarnation into a new life, yet still in full possession of the enlightenment he gained as Gwion. This part of the tale — or at least the belief behind it — is ancient.

I'm not the first, and certainly won't be the last, to make the rather simple observation that reincarnation isn't a part of Christian philosophy, but it was something the Iron Age Celts of Britain believed two thousand years ago. Neither is it an idea that's confined to the sixteenth-century *Tale of Taliesin*, but as we shall discuss in this chapter, several passages in twelfth-century poems draw on a similar belief. This hasn't gone totally unnoticed by Celtic scholars either; John Morris Jones, for example, a founding father of modern Welsh scholarship, once said:

> *Take first Caesar's account of the teaching of the druids, [Bello Gallico, vi, 14] ... : "The chief doctrine of the Druids is that the soul does not perish, but at death passes from one body to another, and this belief they consider a great incentive to courage, since the fear of annihilation may be put aside. They hold many discussions concerning the stars and their movements, about the size of the world and the universe, about nature, and about the power and attributes of the immortal gods." The quotation is trite enough; but anyone who will look at it again and compare it with ... extracts from the mythico-mystical poems of Taliesin, must, I think, be impressed with the light it throws upon them.*[296]

Before coming to the Taliesin material itself, it's worth seeing what other scant remains we have in the Welsh tradition that can shed some light not only on reincarnation but also on transmigration and channelling, related ideas that all grow out of the same basic belief in a durable soul that, after death, can pass into a new body. Yet just as with the references to Annwfn, it's worth stressing how rare these remains are in mediaevel

---

296   John Morris Jones, *Y Cymmrodor: Taliesin* (London 1918), 247-8.

Welsh literature. We are not talking about a common theme by any stretch of the imagination, but a handful of otherwise unrelated texts that are connected in subtle ways. Like contemplating the surviving shards of a broken, incomplete cauldron, trying to piece such ideas together is really at the limits of what can be interpreted. Yet when some of these pieces touch, they do indeed seem to fit one another, no matter how tentatively. If we can allow for some ambiguity, uncertainty, and the ever-present difficulty of translating ancient Welsh texts into modern English, we may find some sense is to be had.

The first of our puzzle pieces is a poem typically known as 'Stanza 48', and it has caused consternation amongst scholars for some time. It's found in the thirteenth-century *Book of Aneirin*, copied down only a few decades before *The Book of Taliesin*. Aneirin was, of course, a near contemporary of the historical Taliesin, and likewise his *Book* preserves all manner of poetry, some that may have been originally composed by him, but all of which was reworked or composed anew by bards during the centuries after his death. The main body of the manuscript comprises poems that commemorate the fallen warriors of the Gododdin[297] tribe that he served. The king of the Gododdin, whose capital was at Edinburgh, feasted hundreds of warriors on mead for an entire year, a feast that was a down-

---

297   God-OTH-in.

payment for an attack on the stronghold of Catterick, held at that time by the Germanic Angles. The tribe's bard, Aneirin, went with the Welsh war-band to witness their heroism in battle. Tragically, the entire force was nearly destroyed. Only Aneirin (and perhaps a few others) survived to commemorate the fallen heroes in a glorious series of elegies known today simply as *Y Gododdin*. But 'Stanza 48' differs from these elegies, even though it mentions the legendary battle and Aneirin by name, which is probably why it was included in *The Book of Aneirin*:

> I'm no weary lord,
>
> I avenge no wrong,
>
> I laugh no laughter.
>
> Under crawlers' feet,
>
> My legs at full length,
>
> In a house of earth,
>
> A chain of iron,
>
> About both ankles.
>
> By mead, by horn,
>
> By the folk of Catterick:
>
> I, not I, Aneirin,
>
> (Taliesin knows it,

Master of word-craft)

I sang to Gododdin

Before the day dawned.[298]

In the first three lines, the poet is telling us he is not a part of the everyday life of the court: he's not a weary lord enduring some boring recital of poetry, he's not a great warrior out and about righting wrongs, neither is he a merrymaker in the mead hall. Instead, he is laid out underground, in some type of subterranean space, perhaps even a burial mound, his ankles bound by an iron chain. Being willingly bound and trapped underground like a corpse looks like a type of symbolic burial and death.[299] If this is the case, it would explain some of the stranger lines in the second half of the poem:

I, not I, Aneirin,

(Taliesin knows it,

Master of word craft).

---

298 My translation of the text in Ifor Williams (ed.), *Canu Aneirin* (UWP 1961), 22.

299 A general discussion from an anthropological perspective can be found in Mircea Eliade, *Rites and Symbols of Initiation: The Mysteries of Birth and Rebirth* (Spring Publications 1994).

We can read this as a type of riddle.[300] Claiming to be and not to be someone can be understood as the condition of containing two personalities at the same time: that is the legendary bard Aneirin and also the speaking bard in the same body. Two personalities occupying one body is a phenomenon we find in many cultures across the world and is usually called channelling or possession, often intentionally practiced by those taking on a priest-like or shamanic role.

The simplest explanation is that this possibly ninth-century bard was claiming to channel, metaphorically or otherwise, the sixth-century Aneirin.[301] Strangely, the statement is made from the position of the channelled Aneirin, as if the dead poet is aware of the fact that it is him, and yet not him, who speaks. This would also mean the symbolic death was necessary for the poem to have been brought about, the anonymous poet having to leave the land of the living before he can speak with the voice of the dead.

---

300   This and later types of riddle in the Welsh tradition echo the words of the 3rd century Greek biographer Diogenes Laertius in *Vitae*, trans. Philip Freeman in *The Celtic Heroic Age*, p. 30: 'Those who believe philosophy arose among the barbarians explain the teachings of each group. They say the Gymnosophists [of India] and Druids instruct by means of riddles, urging worship of the gods, abstinence from evil, and the practice of manly virtue.'

301   Two scholars in particular have suggested similar interpretations of these lines: Patrick K. Ford, 'The Death of Aneirin', *Bulletin of the Board of Celtic Studies* 34 (UWP 1987), 47: 'The implication is that poets must experience an isolation tantamount to death and burial as part of the initiation process — just as in the primordial story of Taliesin, where the initiate was swallowed, lay first in the womb of the mam-awen Ceridwen, then was reborn, then was Taliesin.'; Brendan O Hehir, 'What is the Gododdin?', *Early Welsh Poetry: Studies in the Book of Aneirin* (NLW 1988), 74: 'The speaker, in other words, is a poet whose personal name and identity is not that of Aneirin, but who in the poetic trance assumes the persona of Aneirin, is possessed by the spirit of Aneirin, and composes in the name of Aneirin: 'I am Aneirin who am not.''

The next line, *'Taliesin knows it'* suggests this condition of being channelled is also something that the long-dead Taliesin experiences. This would mean that members of a bardic school that preserved the traditional work of Aneirin and Taliesin were involved in the channelling of these founding fathers. Not only would such a bardic school have ensured the transmission of poetry down the generations, but also enabled its adherents to speak with the channelled voices of their legendary masters, the clear intention being to bring them back from the dead so that they could speak to the living. A comparable idea is found in an old poem where Myrddin (the original Merlin), foretells the future as he speaks from his own grave.[302]

One of the more obvious elements that's found elsewhere in mediaevel Welsh poetry is the '. . . *chain of iron, | About both ankles'* that's binding the poet while he's laid out in a *'house of earth'*. If we cast our minds back to 'The Spoils of Annwfn', we will recall this description of Gwair's condition:

> Before him, no one had gone there —
>
> Into the heavy, grey chain guarding the best of youths.
>
> And he was singing sadly before the spoils of Annwfn,
>
> And our poetic prayer shall continue until Doom.

---

302   An edition of the Welsh text can be found by E.G.B. Phillimore in *Y Cymmrodor* Vol. 7 (1886), 151-4.

Considering that Gwair is also bound by a chain, is connected to bardic utterance, and trapped in Caer Siddi, 'The Fairy-mound Fortress', both texts could be describing the same basic situation in different symbolic terms. Whereas 'Stanza 48' is giving a potentially more literal description of the event, 'The Spoils of Annwfn' would be giving the more symbolic or mythic version. Either way, 'Stanza 48' reads like an account of some mystical experience, perhaps during a bardic ceremony, or at the very least, an imagined situation in which the poet channels Aneirin. And whereas it's tempting to see the poem as a literal description of an actual event, it could likewise be more of a symbolic account of the relationship between living bards and their ancestral masters, learning as they did the words of the dead.

That said, there is one other source that suggests an actual location for such a ritual burial, had one indeed ever been enacted. In one of the long poems recorded by Elis Gruffydd in his version of *The Tale of Taliesin*, during his first tumultuous visit to Maelgwn's court, the young Taliesin says:

> I was in the blessed mound
>
> In the court of Cynfelyn,
>
> In a shackle and chain
>
> for a year and a day . . . [303]

---

303   My translation of the text in Ford (1992), 78.

Here, the bard endures a year and a day bound and shackled, a period that's mentioned often in many folk traditions, describing as it does one complete cycle of the seasons. These few lines also give us a clue to a location.

There is only one 'blessed mound' that's directly connected to Taliesin, and that's Bedd Taliesin, 'Taliesin's Grave', an old burial mound that overlooks the Dyfi Estuary from the south. It's unclear how old it is exactly, but the latest thinking is that it's from the early mediaevel period, around the time of the historical Taliesin, although it's situated very close to similar bronze age monuments. The earliest recorded name for it is Gwely Taliesin, 'Taliesin's Bed', *gwely* often used figuratively to mean grave, but also suggesting a place where anyone could recline. The gentleman-scholar Samuel Meyrick included a scrap of local folklore about the mound in his history of Ceredigion county, published in 1808:

> *The popular superstition respecting this, is that should anyone sleep in this bed for one night, he would the next day become either a poet, or an idiot.*[304]

A similar belief is connected to a few other places,[305] but here it echoes the basic scheme of a ritual period spent in an ancient burial mound so as to spiritually receive a poetic ability. The

---

304   Samuel Meyrick, *The History and Antiquities of the County of Cardigan* (1808), 432.

305   See https://sublimewales.wordpress.com/material-culture/carreg-y-bardd-the-poet-stone/

poem gives us another hint that this blessed mound is indeed Bedd Taliesin by telling us it's in Llys Cynfelyn,[306] 'Cynfelyn's Court'. It just so happens that the mound is only a hundred yards beyond the bounds of the parish of Llangynfelyn, the church itself being less than two miles away on the other side of the village of Tre Taliesin ('Taliesin's Town').

The St Cynfelyn who gave his name to this church was a descendent of Ceredig,[307] the prince that gave his name to the county of Ceredigion where both Bedd Taliesin and Llangynfelyn are located. Cynfelyn lived sometime towards the end of the fifth century, so in historical terms at least, his court may well have been established somewhere near Llangynfelyn parish a few generations before the historical Taliesin was born. Taliesin's grave could well have been on lands once held by Cynfelyn and surrounding his court, traditionally known as *Llys Cynfelyn*.[308]

As mentioned by Patrick Ford in his edition of *Ystoria Taliesin*,[309] there is a further allusion to this type of symbolic burial in the poetry preserved in *The Tale*:

> Low bards of the region,

---

306   Llis Kin-VEL-in.

307   Peter C. Bartrum, *A Welsh Classical Dictionary* (NLW 1993), 175.

308   An assumption also made by local historian Richard James Thomas in his article 'Cynfelyn Sant', *Lloffion Llangynfelyn*, 4 (January 1957), 7-8.

309   Ford (1992), 123-4.

Why do you not flee?

The bard who does not silence me

Shall not have peace

Until he goes into a stillness,

Below pebbles and shale . . .[310]

There are, of course, two ways of understanding these lines. Either the legendary Taliesin is telling the bards at Maelgwn's court that if they cannot best him in a bardic contest, they shall never hear the end of it until the day they die. The other meaning suggested by Ford is that a bard will never have a hope of besting Taliesin until he has also experienced the symbolic death alluded to; that is, becoming a fully initiated bard in the Taliesin tradition.

This suggests the divine awen was much more than a refined type of inspiration, but a spiritual force that allowed the living to commune with the dead. Not only was the inherited poetry of Taliesin and Aneirin a quarry for later bards,[311] but also the means by which they could connect directly with the original source, the mystical voice that spoke in that ancient

---

310   My translation of the text in Ford (1992), 81.

311   Again, we can turn to Caesar's description of druidic learning for a comparable sense of oral education in the preceding period of Celtic culture. *De Bello Gallico* 6.11—20, CHA, p. 14: 'They are said to commit to memory a great number of verses. And they remain some 20 years in training. Nor do they judge it to be allowed to entrust these things to writing although in nearly the rest of their affairs, and public and private transactions, Greek letters are used.'

verse. Such a practice, if taken seriously, would have conferred a priestlike authority on the bards.

Yet even though we have a potential location for this hypothetical ritual, there is no direct evidence to say that any bard ever experienced such a thing. Beyond 'Stanza 48', no other first- or second-hand accounts have ever been found in the Welsh historical record, even though Ford notes several similar practices in related Celtic traditions.[312] But there are a few other observations to be made about the broader landscape around Bedd Taliesin that may at least hint at a ritualised landscape.

In preparation for the birth of our first child in 2012, my wife and I moved to one of the most beautiful places in Wales, Cwm Einion, the valley of the Einion river, a tributary of the Dyfi that flows into the great estuary from the south. It's one of the few places that maintains its temperate rain-forest, once so common in these lands. Its steep hills are covered in oak, birch and rowan woods, where large moss-covered boulders watch over the river deep down in the ravine. Once our son was born, it was a regular pleasure of mine to take him out for a walk in

---

312 Ford (1992), 14-17.

the woods. I would bundle him up in the back carrier and set off to discover the many paths and secret ways of the wooded river valleys south of the Dyfi. Connecting several of these valleys is an ancient highway that runs along the high ground overlooking the estuary, what we call in Wales a Sarn Helen,[313] or what's more commonly known as a 'Roman Road', even though these ways were used long before the Romans got here.

I had known for years that the ancient mound of Bedd Taliesin was about an hour's walk south of Cwm Einion, in Cwm Clettwr, the next river valley along. So, one day I put my tiny son in the back carrier and off we went to find the ancient bard's last resting place. Over the following year, we visited Cwm Clettwr and Bedd Taliesin several times, and I began to wander the surrounding lands, visiting the other nearby cairns, waterfalls and woods. Bedd Taliesin is at a junction between the ancient highway and another old track that joins it from the east called Y Sarn Ddu,[314] 'The Black Road'. They meet at an old farm called Pen-y-sarn-ddu, which can be translated as meaning either 'End of the Black Road' or 'Hill of the Black Road.' Y Sarn Ddu runs east up Cwm Clettwr, past Bedd Taliesin and through another old farm called Cae'r Arglwyddes, then continues up the slope of Moel-y-Llyn mountain at the head of the valley, through the *bwlch* ('pass') and down into the head

---

313 See 'The Dream of the Emperor Maxen' in Davies (2007).

314 Uh Sarn Thee.

of Cwm Einion. I had ambitions to walk the whole route up and over into Cwm Einion, then follow the river home. I often ventured up Y Sarn Ddu, seeing how far we could get before Dad's legs began to tire, and always gave up long before we got to Cae'r Arglwyddes farm.

Even though Y Sarn Ddu disappears at the pass, if you follow the steep hill down on the other side of Moel-y-Llyn mountain, you reach a small farmstead called Bronwion, 'Gwion's Hill'. I really wanted to get to Bronwion because it had occurred to me that it could be connected somehow to Bedd Taliesin.

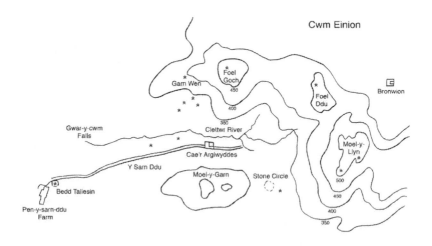

Alas, for about a year I had to be content with exploring Cwm Clettwr, which is littered with piles of stones, some of which are assumed to be the result of farmers clearing ground for new pasture. At least two of the piles have been identified as cairns ('burial mounds'), and they have several big quartz stones in them, some as large as small boulders. When I eventually made it up to the hills surrounding Cwm Clettwr (without the boy on my back this time), I discovered the very distinct quartz 'cap' on the cairn on Moel-y-Llyn and the quartz boulders that kerb the cairns on the overlooking Foel Goch mountain.

It appears the bronze age cairn builders favoured the white shining rocks. Many of the apparently random piles of stones in the fields surrounding the old farm of Cae'r Arglwyddes also contain large quartz stones, which leads me to assume that they are also the remains of cairns. If this is the case, there were several burials here for people important enough to have quartz decorated graves. Along Y Sarn Ddu, there are also several fallen standing stones, most of which clearly mark the old way. Cwm Clettwr may have once been the site of a burial complex through which 'The Black Road' ran, perhaps once functioning as a processional route through the mounds.

And what of the name Cae'r Arglwyddes, 'The Lady's Field'? After some digging around in the National Library and County Archive, I am yet to discover if it was ever owned by a noblewoman. But perhaps the most intriguing possibility is that these named sites along Y Sarn Ddu correspond with the mythical bard's life-journey. If so, this would explain who this lady is. In the tale, Ceridwen stands between Gwion and

Taliesin, just as Cae'r Arglwyddes, 'The Lady's Field', stands between Bronwion, 'Gwion's Hill', and Bedd Taliesin, 'Taliesin's Grave', all connected by Y Sarn Ddu, 'The Black Road'. Perhaps in the imagination of local folk at least, Cwm Clettwr was where Ceridwen chased the magically enlightened Gwion Bach, a place already laden with connotations of death and rebirth.

Or perhaps this was the site of a ritual procession where apprentice bards were initiated into the mysteries of Ceridwen, beginning their journey at Bronwion, taking Y Sarn Ddu through the pass into Cwm Clettwr, through Cae'r Arglwyddes, and eventually coming to their symbolic death at Bedd Taliesin. Again, we have no evidence for such a ritual beyond the brief allusions in the texts we've discussed, and what may be nothing more than a lucky coincidence of place names. But taken all together, they are suggestive, especially considering this is the area where the events of one of the earliest recorded versions of *The Tale of Taliesin* took place.

A similar arrangement of stories, places, and histories can be found at the end of the Conwy Valley in North Wales, which is the river estuary where Taliesin is reborn in the Elis Gruffydd version, the Dyfi estuary being where John Jones' 1607 version is set. Overlooking the Conwy estuary is the old site of Deganwy Castle, where Maelgwn Gwynedd had his court in the early sixth century and which was also fortified by Llywelyn the Great in the thirteenth. In the earliest version of his legend, it was a place the young Taliesin had words with Maelgwn's bards and released his patron, Elffin, from prison. It was also frequented by Llywarch ap Llywelyn, court bard to Llywelyn the Great and potential author or adapter of many of the legendary poems in *The Book of Taliesin*.

A few miles to the south of where Deganwy Castle once stood runs another ancient coastal highway, crossing the mouth of the Conwy and heading up into the mountains of northern Eryri. All along this old track there are many cairns, standing stones and other Neolithic and bronze age constructions, including the magnificent twin menhir of Bwlch y Ddeufaen, 'The Pass of Two Stones'. Within this complex of ancient monuments are the remnants of a chambered cairn once covered in a mound of earth that has since disappeared, revealing a small stone chamber still roofed with a large slab. This perfectly proportioned stone 'hut' is called Maen y Bardd,[315] 'The Bard's Stone', again a very suggestive name considering the area's connections to the legendary Taliesin and those who once promoted his myth.

315   Mine uh Barth.

The Dyfi and Conwy estuaries are the settings for both of the oldest surviving versions of *The Tale of Taliesin*. Overlooking each estuary is an ancient coastal highway, around which is situated a large complex of ancient stone monuments, one of which is a 'house of earth', named especially for its connection to a bard. What springs to mind is the possibility of the same basic rites of initiation practiced in two similar places, as if the bardic schools in each area (or perhaps the same school in both), required a certain type of landscape with an ancient monument suitable for a symbolic death. There are no actual accounts of any such rites being held, but such things may well have been hidden from sight. At the very least, the Taliesin myth of reincarnation found a home in two very similar landscapes where we find ancient monuments built for the dead.

As the longest poem in *The Book of Taliesin*, it's perhaps unsurprising that 'Angar Kyfundawt', 'The Hostile Confederacy', touches on all the more important themes in Taliesin's myth. As a poem that may also have been performed at Deganwy Castle, either by Llywarch ap Llywelyn himself or one of his apprentices, it is fittingly set in a contest between Taliesin and a 'hostile confederacy' of opposing bards. There are two types of occasion on which this poem may have been performed, either at an actual bardic competition or before the gathered court as part of an evening's entertainment. In both cases, the performing bard would have adopted the dramatic persona of the legendary Taliesin, and in the opening scene he puts his competitor, imagined or otherwise, in his place:

> Here is the poet!
>
> I've sung already what he'll sing.
>
> He'll sing when
>
> The sage has finished wherever he may be.
>
> A patron who refuses me
>
> Will get nothing to give.
>
> Through Taliesin's language
>
> The profit of manna.

> When Cian died
>
> His retinue was large.[316]

Taliesin addresses not only his opponent but the noble patron who's probably supplying the hall and the drink. The basic claim here is that if the patron wants to be successful, if he wants to win glory and fame, he should give patronage to Taliesin. With such a wise and talented sage at his side, how could he not succeed? To prove how successful great bards can be, Taliesin mentions Cian, a chief bard of ancient history who was so successful he had a large retinue of followers.

In the next section, things get a bit more mysterious:

> Until death it shall be [. . .],
>
> The declamation of Afagddu:
>
> He brought forth skilfully
>
> Speech in poetic metre.[317]

Unfortunately, the scribe failed to copy the end of the first line, so we can only really guess what the missing word would have been. Regardless, we have a connection between death and the 'declamation of Afagddu'. This is another name for Morfran in the sixteenth-century *Tale of Taliesin*, that being

---

316 My translation of the text in Haycock (2015), 110.

317 Ibid. 110-1.

Ceridwen's son, the one who should have got the potion of inspiration before Gwion Bach took his place at the cauldron. Yet the Afagddu in this twelfth-century poem appears to have received that magical inspiration and is now himself a great bard. Even though there are plenty of similarities between the earlier *Book* and the later *Tale*, as discussed earlier, neither is it surprising to find differences.

Even though the mention of death is obscure, it continues in the next section, where we may make some little sense of it:

> Gwion speaks —
>
> And a deep one will come;
>
> He makes the dead live, . . .[318]

All three bards, Cian, Afagddu and Gwion seem to possess great bardic power, and are named here as a proof of why noblemen should give patronage to their tradition. Cian attracts a great following, Afagddu is supremely skilled in bardic speech and Gwion can bring the dead to life.

Gwion's character here is at least similar in the later folktale, and as we'd expect of someone who drank from the cauldron of inspiration, his bardic declamations have a

---

318   Ibid. Notice that my translation of the word *dwfn* differs from Haycock's in that I believe an Annwfn depth is more in keeping with the subject matter than the more general 'profound' given by Haycock. See my note 'Annwfn ac Awen Rhai o'r Gofynfeirdd', *Dwned* (Aberystwyth, 2015), 111-4.

supernatural power. He can apparently invoke a 'deep one' from Annwfn simply by reciting poetry. Not only that, but Gwion can also bring the dead to life, the implication being that both statements describe the same act: through the act of declaiming awen-inspired verse, a deep one from Annwfn is brought back to life. The bard here appears to be alluding to the practice of channelling, the implication being that just as Gwion Bach transformed into the legendary Taliesin, the performing bard also transforms into the great master, bringing him back to life through the declamation of enchanted verse.

There are two other lines in the opening section of 'The Hostile Confederacy' which chime with this meaning. In lines 23-24 we read *'Song will be brought forth passionately / By the deep declaimer of verse'*,[319] and then more explicitly in lines 31-35:

> When all are sifted out,
>
> I'll come with the poetry
>
> Of a deep one who became flesh:
>
> A conqueror has come,
>
> A third ready judge.[320]

---

319   My translation of the text in Haycock (2015), 111.

320   Ibid.

Poetry is the medium through which a deep one from Annwfn becomes flesh. If so, the performer becomes the 'deep one' Taliesin, the speaking persona shifting to that of the legendary Taliesin in the performance of the poem, just as Aneirin is the bard who is not Aneirin in 'Stanza 48.' If these lines in any way reflect the beliefs of twelfth-century court bards, their tradition was more pagan than we have otherwise guessed.

This belief in the ability of bards to channel the voice of Taliesin appears to persist. It would at least explain one of the more mysterious couplets we've already looked at, that being from Dafydd Epynt's 1480 eulogy for a fellow bard:

> He casts aside his spear [and the] four elements,
>
> He tends the silk of Cadair Sidydd.
>
> A name was upon his lips for the voice of Taliesin
>
> In a blessed way for our awenydd.

The dead bard appears to have gone to Cadair Sidydd at death, and just like the poet who gave us the legendary poems, he also speaks with the voice of the ancient master. More intriguing yet is the practice alluded to, the poet apparently using a special name to invoke Taliesin's voice, and that this practice was a type of blessing for this *awenydd*.[321]

---

321 Aw-EN-ith.

Awenydd is generally used as a term for a poet, but considering what else is being spoken of here, Dafydd Epynt may be using it in a very specific way. One of the earliest references we have to an *awenydd* can be found in the twelfth-century writings of Gerald of Wales, that terrible mediaeval gossip who disparaged not only the Welsh but the Irish as he travelled their lands, gathering juicy tidbits for his Anglo-Norman audience. Even though we must take what he says with a pinch of salt, there may well be some kernel of truth in his description of the Welsh *awenyddion*[322] (plural of *awenydd*). The text quoted below, *The Description of Wales*, was written by Gerald during the 1190s, a period when legendary poems such as 'The Hostile Confederacy' were possibly being reworked and performed:

> *Among the Welsh there are certain individuals called 'awenyddion' who behave as if they are possessed by devils. You will not find them anywhere else. When you consult them about some problem, they immediately go into a trance and lose control of their senses, as if they are possessed. They do not answer the question put to them in any logical way. Words stream from their mouths, incoherently and apparently meaningless and without any sense at all, but all the same well expressed: and if you listen carefully to what they say you will receive the solution to your problem. When it is all over, they will recover from their trance, as if they were ordinary people*

---

322 Awen-UTH-ion.

waking from a heavy sleep, but you have to give them
a good shake before they regain control of themselves.
There are two odd things about all this: when they
have given their answer, they do not recover from their
paroxysm unless they are shaken violently and forced
to come round again; and when they do return to their
senses they can remember nothing of what they have said
in the interval. If by chance they are questioned a second
or a third time on the same matter, they give completely
different answers. It is possible that they are speaking
through demons which possess them, spirits which are
ignorant and yet in some way inspired. They seem to
receive this gift of divination through visions which they
see in their dreams. Some of them have the impression that
honey or sugary milk is being smeared on their mouths;
others say that a sheet of paper with words written on it
is pressed against their lips. As soon as they are roused
from their trance and have come round again after their
prophesying, that is what they say has happened.[323]

Apparently, an *awenydd* was someone who could be possessed by spirits, perhaps those of the dead. This may well be the meaning Dafydd Epynt was referring to, considering the 'voice of Taliesin' that his dead comrade appeared to be able speak with. Taken with the other poems looked at so far in this chapter, the implication here is that at least from the ninth century through to the fifteenth, certain lineages in the Welsh

---

323   Lewis Thorpe (trans.), *The Journey through Wales and The Description of Wales* (Penguin 2004), 246.

bardic tradition practiced a type of channelling where the voices of ancient bardic masters were invoked in performance. In the more extreme cases, as with the description of the *awenyddion*, this could have become a full possession. The basic belief appears to have been that immortal souls such as Taliesin resided in Annwfn and that their voices could be transmitted to the living through the divine inspiration of awen.

Such beliefs have been part of the broader European tradition for a very long time.[324] A description very similar to Gerald's *awenyddion* was given fifteen hundred years earlier in one of Plato's dialogues on inspiration:

> ... the authors of those great poems which we admire, do not attain to excellence through the rules of any art, but they utter their beautiful melodies of verse in a state of inspiration, and, as it were, possessed by a spirit not their own. Thus the composers of lyrical poetry create those admired songs of theirs in a state of divine insanity, like the Corybantes, who lose all control over their reason in the enthusiasm of the sacred dance: and, during this supernatural possession, are excited to the rhythm and harmony which they communicate to men.[325]

Beliefs such as these were common in the Greek culture of two and a half millennia ago, and echo those held by cousin

---

324   See C. M. Bowra, *Inspiration and Poetry* (London, 1955), Chapter 1.

325   Plato, 'Ion', A. D. Lindsay (ed.), *Five Dialogues of Plato Bearing Upon Inspiration* (London 1910), 6.

cultures on the Indo-European family tree, including the Italic, Germanic and Celtic. The essential concept is of a power emanating from the otherworld, which becomes irresistible to the mortal, causing them to respond bodily to the supernatural force. They become a portal through which the otherworld enters our own, and being overwhelmed by its eternal nature, the poet overflows with an outpouring of strange utterances.

To return to Wales, a hundred years after Gerald wrote his account of the *awenyddion*, a court bard by the name of Iorwerth Fychan described himself declaiming praise: '*I become ecstatic; I praise like an awenydd . . .*'[326] The ecstatic nature of possession by the *awenyddion* was at least comparable to the way a court bard was possessed by the inspiration of Annwfn. The bard had one foot firmly in the court while also being present to the reality of the inner deep. The ambiguity of where the bard actually stood in the moment they were possessed by awen was a part of their mystique. For some, at least, their spiritual authority was a consequence of their ability to unite this world and the inner deep, where time is not the same. If Annwfn is where the immortal souls of bardic masters reside, then as a living bard bridges the divide, those ancient ones can come through to be reborn in performance on the mortal plane.

---

326   My translation of the text in Brynley F. Roberts et al (eds.), *Gwaith Bleddyn Fardd a beirdd eraill . . .* (UWP 1996), 324.

The broader culture of Christianity had been influencing Taliesin's myth since the earliest stages of its evolution. As we have already seen, the legendary poems in *The Book of Taliesin* often contain a heady mix of Christian and pagan mysticism. This Christian influence continued in Elis Gruffydd's sixteenth-century version of *The Tale of Taliesin*, but not always the better part of Christianity, either. *The Tale* can be read as an early modern rendition of a pagan mythology, but neither should it be forgotten that Gruffydd reworked parts of the story to abide by the Christian norms of his day, some of which are discriminatory and a few just plain evil.

Even though these elements are relatively superficial compared to the mythological foundations of the tale, they are still a part of Gruffydd's version. Those that come under the lash in his text include wandering minstrels, Jews,[327] women and poor land workers,[328] all of whom lived with various forms of oppression and discrimination. Even though this isn't the place to delve into these attitudes, before we explore the

---

327   One later section of poetry in *The Tale* is particularly bad, where Taliesin says of lower class minstrels: '*Everything seeks its* [*own*] *food,* / *Apart from minstrels and lazy thieves and worthless Jews.*' My translation of the text in Ford (1992), 81.

328   According to an apocryphal tradition mentioned in a poem in *The Tale* (Ford, 83-6), Eve, the original sinner, stole some seeds given by an angel intended for planting. As a result, the Church claimed everybody should give a tenth, a 'tithe', of their produce to the Church because all are party to Eve's original sin. This was effectively a Church tax on poor people, and it's an idea smuggled into one of the later poems in *The Tale*.

Christian influence in Gruffydd's version of *The Tale*, neither should such attitudes be totally ignored, as they so often are.

Perhaps the most obvious place Gruffydd's Christianity can be seen in *The Tale* is where any other type of belief becomes too apparent. For example, Gruffydd's distaste at the obvious paganism of the story:

> *And truly, this story is irrational and against faith and sanctity. Nevertheless, as before, the body of the story shows clearly that [Ceridwen] gathered a great many of the Earth's plants, and these she put in a cauldron of water, that she put on the fire.*[329]

His opinion has been inserted just before the explicit description of Ceridwen acting as a witch, stressing the fact that he wasn't an author seeking esoteric, pagan knowledge, even if he was attracted to the more acceptable mysticism of the Welsh bardic tradition. We can still be relatively confident he recounted the traditional tale as it agrees with other sources, but neither was Gruffydd able to give a totally neutral account of the myth.

Another very Christian perspective that's given in *The Tale* has its origins in the earliest period of the faith in Britain. Gildas was a sixth-century Welsh monk who wrote a document called *De Excidio Britanniae*, '*On the Ruin of Britain*'. It's a sermon on the downfall of the Welsh, blamed on the

---

329   My translation of the text in Ford (1992), 66.

sinfulness of Welsh kings and the failings of the Welsh clergy. God punished the Welsh for their sins by giving Britain to the Germanic invaders. Gildas was a contemporary of Maelgwn Gwynedd, one of the main characters in *The Tale of Taliesin*, and he addresses the Welsh king directly in his sermon:

> *Thou does not listen to the praises of God, sweetly sounded forth by the pleasant voices of Christ's soldiers, nor the instruments of ecclesiastical melody.*[330]

Instead, Maelgwn listens to ...

> *... thine own praises, which are nothing, rung after the fashion of the giddy route of Bacchus, by the mouths of thy villainous followers, accompanied with lies and malice.*[331]

Gildas is talking about Maelgwn's court bards, defining a stereotype that persists down the centuries, appearing in the twelfth-century legendary poems and in the sixteenth-century *Tale of Taliesin*.

Of course, any text can express more than one meaning, and just as the more discriminatory and judgmental parts of Christian culture permeate the folktale, so do the more mystical elements of the faith, often combined with the native mysticism of the bards. The episode that most clearly reveals a similarity between Christian and pagan myth is the rebirth scene itself. An infant set upon a river, who remains adrift

---

330   J. A. Giles & T. Habington (trans.), *Gildas' 'On the Ruin of Britain'* (1842), 25.

331   Ibid.

for forty years, is the basic story of Moses, and Elis Gruffydd appears to have been consciously evoking the Old Testament story in his rendition.[332] Especially as sixty years appears to be the period mentioned in the earlier legendary poems,[333] Gruffydd's forty brings Taliesin's tale further into alignment with that of Moses. But perhaps the most striking example is the conflation of Taliesin's rebirth with Christian resurrection. In the very first line of poetry declaimed by the young Taliesin before Maelgwn, he says:

> A common chief bard am I to Elffin,
>
> And my homeland is the land of the Cherubim.

In Patrick Ford's edition of the text, he reads the 'land of the Cherubim' as a reference to a passage in The Book of Enoch, written between 300 and 200 BCE:

> There was a wise man, a great artificer, and the Lord conceived love for him, and received him, so that he should behold the uppermost dwellings, and be an eyewitness of the wise and great and inconceivable, and immutable realm of God Almighty.[334]

---

332 See Amy C. Mulligan, 'Moses, Taliesin, and the Welsh Chosen People: Elis Gruffydd's Construction of a Biblical, British Past for Reformation Wales', *Studies in Philology* Vol. 113, No. 4 (2016), 765-796.

333 Haycock (2015), 111-2, my translation: 'For sixty years / I bore solitude / In water . . .'

334 Rutherford H. Platt, Jr. (trans.), *The Forgotten Books of Eden* (1926), 81.

This wise artificer, Enoch, is taken up to heaven before he dies and is witness to

> . . . *the various apparitions and inexpressible singing of*
> *the host of Cherubim.*[335]

Ford's assumption is that the Welsh bards knew of the apocryphal texts concerning Enoch and readily drew on their mystical influence.[336] This allusion in Taliesin's poem does at least present the possibility that it was known in Wales, and Ford assumes that Taliesin and Enoch were seen as being very similar, both *'privy to the secrets of the universe.'*[337]

A similar blending can be found elsewhere in the poems of *The Tale*:

> Johan the Wizard called me Myrddin,
>
> But now every king calls me Taliesin.[338]

According to Ford, *'Johan the Wizard'* could be John the Baptist who heralded the coming of Christ. By recognising the reincarnating Welsh spirit in one of his earlier lives as Myrddin, John is performing a similar role in the Welsh myth:

---

335   Ibid. 82.

336   Ford (1992), 52-3.

337   Ibid. 114.

338   My translation of the text in Ford (1992), 76.

> *Our poet would seem to claim that it was also John's*
> *role to identify him, the secular logos, or the secular*
> *manifestation of God's word in the mortal realm.*
> *Although, in those days he went by the name Myrddin, in*
> *other words, John and Myrddin, that is Taliesin, are of the*
> *same brotherhood, the masters of Prophetic Visionary*
> *and symbolic wisdom.*[339]

We can, of course, take this a step further. It's not just that John the Baptist and Myrddin and Taliesin are part of the same brotherhood, there is also an explicit projection of Taliesin onto the figure of Jesus himself:

> *And then King Maelgwn asked him where he had been,*
> *and he told this story to the king, as follows in this work:*

> I was with my Lord in the heights
>
> When Lucifer fell to the depths of Hell.
>
> I led with a standard before Alexander the Great,
>
> And I know the names of the stars from north to south.
>
> I was in Gwydion's fort, with Tetragrammaton.[340]

Tetragrammaton is the name of God, sometimes Jesus in Renaissance Kabbalah, a name so sacred it was forbidden to be uttered. A secret vocalisation of the ultimate supernatural

---

339   Ford (1992), 114.

340   My translation of the text in Ford (1992), 76-7. I've amended the meaning of the last line in keeping with another manuscript version. See Ford's notes, 115.

power would have been a tempting concept for Welsh bardic mystics, especially considering the power conferred upon those who knew such esoteric words. There is clearly a mixing of native and Christian mythology here in God's secret name being known in Gwydion's Fort.[341] The next section of the poem continues in much the same vein:

> Then I was in Canaan when Absalom was killed.
>
> I brought seeds to the Vale of Hebron.
>
> I was in the court of noblemen before the birth of Gwydion.
>
> I was a patriarch to Eli and Enoch.
>
> I was chief keeper of the works of Nimrod Tower
>
> When all the languages of the world were one.
>
> I was upon the cross of God's compassionate son.[342]

The Vale of Hebron was abundant, and Taliesin claims he was the first to bring seeds to the place. He was also the foreman who built the Tower of Babel, perhaps a fitting role for a master of language such as Taliesin. The last line is the most intriguing by far, as it suggests that Taliesin was with Jesus on the cross, or was in fact 'God's compassionate son', implying they are both

341 Perhaps itself another name for Annwfn or The Milky Way, or both at the same time? See the folktale recorded by John Jones of Gellilyfdy, noted by W.J. Gruffydd, *Math fab Mathonwy* (UWP 1928), 199, where The Milky Way is called Caergwydion while also being the place Lleu's soul is found.

342 My translation of the text in Ford (1992), 77.

one and the same. There is a great deal of similarity between the basic myth of Jesus and that of Taliesin: both are spirit made flesh, supernature made manifest in the mortal realm; both live and die like mortals, but also live on as immortal souls; both bring a divine wisdom into the world to better the lot of their fellow humans.

Of course, to come out and say explicitly that Taliesin is the Welsh Jesus would have been blasphemy in Gruffydd's day, as it still is in some quarters. Yet the basic similarity remains, and it has a certain logic in terms of cultural politics. For all the Church's active opposition to anything that contradicted Christian dogma, as ubiquitous a myth as Taliesin's was clearly impossible to eliminate. Sometimes it's far better to appropriate and absorb than to attack head on.

Neither was the final identification of Taliesin with Jesus necessarily intentional. In the imagination of some, there may have already been a natural blending of both mythic figures; the similarities between the two would surely not have been lost on the more perceptive. This may have been further compounded as the more literate class, Elis Gruffydd amongst them, came to develop their own, more Christian telling of Taliesin's tale, even if they unknowingly preserved the pagan foundations of the myth in doing so.

It's not difficult to see how Taliesin and Jesus were drawn into each other's orbits. Yet in the end, the one isn't the other.

The great saviour of the Christian tradition was resurrected for very specific religious reasons, whereas Taliesin's own countless births, deaths, transmigrations and transformations do not appear to have had such a goal. For mediaevel Christians, the soul was on a one-way journey, either up or down, but for Taliesin the journey just kept going round and around. It's not even clear if the soul in the Christian sense fits into the scheme of Taliesin's myth. For all of the attempt to make it work, there is a fundamental difference between the reincarnating centre of awareness that is Taliesin and the anchor of salvation that is Jesus. They have different aims in their respective mythologies, no matter how much they can be made to overlap.

Another basic difference is in the tone of each myth. Christianity is focused on the crisis of the sinful soul, where joy is found in salvation and entry into heaven. Taliesin, on the other hand, presents a vision of the eternal soul continuously embroiled in the diverse manifestations of creation. There surely is suffering, terror and pain as life is pursued and inevitably caught in the jaws of death, yet in the transformations this enables there is also wonder, intensity and passion. Taliesin's joy is found in the innumerable perspectives granted by physical being, be that as inanimate as a block or as vigorous as a stallion in stud. Jesus is a balm to the awful temptations of the body, whereas Taliesin appears to revel in its very nature. In this, there is a difference between the two mythologies.

Christianity directs its gaze beyond the material realm in hope of ascending to the eternal, the pure and the timeless. Taliesin on the other hand, celebrates the conjunction of these realms as he frolics in material existence. Both spiritual philosophies acknowledge a temporal, physical realm existing alongside a timeless, immaterial dimension, but they describe very different relationships between the two. Where the Augustinian Church in particular seeks to separate them and position one above the other, the native Welsh myth finds the timeless entangled with the temporal, and in Taliesin's case, it is a full and merry entanglement.

On the one hand, he is the great transformer, the ever shifting gaze that skips, flows and hops from one mundane form to another: a droplet in a shower, then a string on a harp, now a bridge, an eagle or a book. On the other hand he is an eternal spirit that incarnates under different guises and names, and when he's not being wise on the mortal plane he lives in the splendid fortress of immortals. Yet he is always, at heart, the divine awen, the conjoining of temporal and timeless, arising from the inner deep to play in the light.

Epilogue

One of the largest national festivals in Wales is the Urdd[343] eisteddfod, a celebration of our young people as they compete in the different arts, including music, literature and theatre. It's open to anyone under 25 years of age and ranges from local preliminary competitions, to regional tiers and then the national competition for all of the regional winners. Our own children did well in the local competition, the eisteddfod cylch,[344] this year; our son coming first for reciting poetry and our daughter second place for singing.

I remember my own nerve-racking experiences on school stages, singing and reciting for audiences of hopeful and supportive teachers, parents and grandparents. The Urdd eisteddfod is one of the main ways we renew our language in these days of an ubiquitous Anglo-American culture that pervades all aspects of our children's lives.

---

343   Irth.

344   Ay-STETH-vod Killch.

This year at the Urdd, as in every other significant eisteddfod, a ceremony was held to honour the winner of the poetry competition. The prize is always a grand chair, a bardic throne, made especially for the occasion, more of a modern work of art these days and usually bequeathed by a carpenter or carpentry company. The 'chairing' is always the highpoint of any such festival and it's carried out with great fanfare and watched by a large audience, live and on television.

All of the most important Welsh language poets of the last few hundred years have been involved in such competitions in one way or another, either as judges or competitors, and it's considered one of the most important institutions in modern Welsh culture, regardless of which eisteddfod the chairing takes place at. At the Urdd eisteddfod this year they tried something new for the first time. Or was it something old?

As the chairing ceremony began, a wrought iron vessel symbolising a cauldron was placed at the centre of the stage; then six young people dressed in colourful animal costumes approached through the audience, each carrying green sprigs of local foliage. As they ascended to the stage they each approached the cauldron and placed their sprigs within it. As they did so, a poem was read out over the sound system that concluded with the words:

We go with magic foliage,

Corn of the field, and blueberry flowers,

Cut and collect beach rushes

And the nettles of our wizardry,

Bring strawberries and the white lily

To put in the Cauldron of Awen.

It was only then that the audience was ready to hear the adjudication of the judges and bear witness to the competition winner sitting upon her bardic throne, honoured and celebrated. The animals were, of course, Ceridwen's representatives, gathering the herbs and placing them in the cauldron. Yet, as each animal was a young person thus transformed, they were also like Gwion Bach.

This was a ceremony held as part of the pomp and pageantry of the festival, consciously drawing on an ancient myth concerning the very Welsh pursuit of awen and the arts. This, amongst countless other instances of poetry, art and music produced in the last decades, show it to be a living myth for Welsh speakers, no matter how secular its expression.

This ceremony — the chairing of a new bard — embodies the primary faith in our own renewal. Just as the great Taliesin is reborn through the magic of awen, brought to life time and again in the imaginations of Welsh audiences, so our young artists come time and again, thankfully, to grace the stage.

Each chairing is a celebration of that perennial power to create anew, to fashion something that has never been before. It may be an ancient and traditional concept, but it's utterly novel in its purest expression, and powerfully optimistic. To create, especially in an old language vying for its very life,[345] is an act of hope if ever there was one, and the renewal of this miracle in every generation gives us a powerful optimism. To know our own children will create, develop, invent and build anew is one of the most heartening things I know.

In simple terms, this is a response to time itself. At risk of sounding utterly banal, things change. The future cannot be known, which means there is no certainty in our continuation as a people, never mind a human race. This anxiety can sometimes be felt just below the surface at large events such as an eisteddfod. As we come together to acknowledge and celebrate our collective expression through the arts, it's unavoidable that we would also be reminded of the slow decline of our language.

It's in those moments that these chairing ceremonies have such great power, as we sanctify our communal voice in the face of that uncertain future. And Taliesin is the perfect metaphor for such moments, as he conveys an innate certainty in the face of undeniable change. In his countless transformations and past

---

345   Over the last century the number of Welsh speakers has declined dramatically from around 900,000 in 1921 to 538,300 in 2021. Since the 2011 census there has been another decline, with the percentage of Welsh speakers dropping from 19.1% of the population in 2011 to 17.9% in 2021. https://www.gov.wales/welsh-language-wales-census-2021-html.

lives, he does not shy away from unavoidable transformation. His confidence tells us that whatever comes it will be experienced to the full. And neither does our legendary bard have any sense of despair in the loss of an old self. He moves forward into the next experience with wit and grace, with power and joy. It's the experience itself, the presence of the moment, that counts, and in that we root ourselves in the creative power of renewal.

This is fundamentally the position of all artists, to bear witness not only to the ever changing world, but to cherish their unique perspective on it, transmitting it in a way that reminds the rest of us how powerful this recurring awen is. In the legendary poems, all phenomena are within Taliesin's grasp; all possible permutations of life can be touched and understood; nothing is beyond the ken of the inspired mind; no corner of creation will remain dark for long under the gaze of the eternally curious poet.

The mediaevel mysticism that found expression in this myth was, in essence, one of poetic vision. But it was not so much the visions themselves that these bards sought, but the perspective from which those visions were experienced, the perspective of the legendary Taliesin himself, the voice that spoke the poetry. Ultimately, Taliesin's myth is concerned with the enduring nature of the voice. It holds that the words of the dead can be spoken by the living, and in doing so, the living bring the dead back into the moments of their lives.

Neither is this some morbid mysticism, but an awareness of the simple nature of language itself. Every one of us only ever speaks words inherited from ancestors, either our own or those of an adopted people. Every time any of us opens our mouths we speak words given to us by countless generations of people who preceded us. Yes, those words are changed, like river stones made smooth by the eternal waters, but they are still the same stone. We are always literally speaking the words of the dead; in our voices, their voices can be heard if we have wit enough to hear them. There is nothing mysterious about inheriting a language, dialect or regional accent, never mind ways of speaking, sayings and phrases cherished by families and friends alike.

For one who speaks Welsh and strives to give it to our children, I cannot fail to see in Taliesin's myth an expression of faith in our own transformative power as a people. This isn't an abstract faith in a distant power which only intervenes in our lives in unknown and unacknowledged ways. Instead, this is a faith that the very words in our mouths continue beyond our own lifetimes, seeking out new tongues to speak them, new understandings to be changed by. Our voice transcends any one generation, perennially arising out of a desire to experience this world.

*An Appendix of Texts, including full translations
of many of the poems discussed in this book,
alongside other additional resources,
videos and lectures can be found at*

https://celticsource.online/taliesin-origins